# PIONEER SPIRIT

# PIONEER SPIRIT

*Modern-day Stories of Courage and Conviction*

## HEIDI S. SWINTON

Deseret Book Company
Salt Lake City, Utah

Library of Congress Cataloging-in-Publication Data

Swinton, Heidi S.,1948–
    Pioneer spirit : modern-day stories of courage and conviction / by
    Heidi S. Swinton.
        p.    cm.
    Includes bibliographical references (p.    ) and index.
    ISBN 1-57345-192-4
    1. Mormons—Biography. 2. Church of Jesus Christ of Latter-day
    Saints—Biography. I. Title.
    BX8693.S95        1996
    289.3'092'2—dc20                                              96-22570
    [B]                                                              CIP
Printed in the United States of America

10   9   8   7   6   5   4   3   2   1

# CONTENTS

Contents

# COURAGE AND DILIGENCE

# PATIENCE AND CHARITY

# Contents

# HUMILITY AND OBEDIENCE

# INTRODUCTION

"Come to Zion" was the gathering call to the Saints in the early days of the Church. And come they did, from England and neighboring European nations, from Nauvoo and Winter Quarters. Some crossed oceans, most journeyed across the plains, and they settled in the Salt Lake Valley and a host of other communities throughout the sprawling territory of Deseret. That pioneer spirit—their belief in the restoration of the gospel of Jesus Christ and their desire to live it in its fulness—is what brought them together. This gathering shaped a spiritual heritage that is being extended by pioneers around the world today.

Modern-day pioneers do not travel to Zion by wagon trains and ox teams, or endure starvation and bitter weather on the plains of Wyoming. But they face journeys of a lifetime just the same. They are the first members of the Church in their home-lands or families; they learn and then teach the gospel in many languages and nations; they are the congregations that stand as one to sing "The Spirit of God" in the dedication of a new temple; they are the faithful who sometimes feel they trudge through daily living, their experiences their own pioneer footprints in the sandy soil of secular society. All are guided by the Lord, who said, "I will

1

take you one of a city, and two of a family, and I will bring you to Zion." (Jeremiah 3:14.)

Pioneers are those who walk a difficult trail to distant frontiers. Gospel pioneers are those who break new ground, who press forward into a wilderness believing fervently that they are building the kingdom of God and that God is directing the way.

Brigham Young told the Saints in 1856: "I tell you the person that keeps his eye upon the mark never considers what he passes through . . . whether it be in walking and pulling handcarts or traveling on foot, going without food and shelter, wandering to and fro, to labor for the people." (Journal History, 5 Oct. 1856, LDS Church Historical Department, Salt Lake City, Utah.)

Pioneers do not set out to be heroes. Yet, they become examples to those who follow because they carry on by applying righteous principles. For the most part, they are good people quietly doing their part. Said President Young to those preparing to cross the plains in one of the early companies, "I just do the thing that I know to be right and the Lord blesses me." (Thomas Bullock Journal, 8 Mar. 1847, LDS Church Historical Department.)

Our pioneer heritage is yoked to distinguishing traits that characterize a latter-day Zion people. Those strengths were described by the Lord to Joseph Smith in 1829:

"O ye that embark in the service of God, see that ye serve him with all your heart, might, mind and strength. . . . And faith, hope, charity and love, with an eye single to the glory of God, qualify him for the work. Remember faith, virtue, knowledge, temperance, patience, brotherly kindness, godliness, charity, humility, diligence." (D&C 4:2, 5–6.)

It was with faith that William Atkin and his wife approached the Green River with their handcart only to find that the wagon train they were with had already crossed and gone on. Turning to his wife, William said, "We cannot cross this river alone." She responded, "No, but the Lord will help us over."

It was with courage that Stillman Pond struggled on to Winter Quarters in 1846, having lost his wife and all nine of his children to "fever and chills" in the four exhausting months since they had fled Nauvoo in the dead of winter.

It was with patience that handcart pioneer John Jacques wrote in his journal on Thursday, 9 October 1856: "You felt you could almost eat a rusty nail or gnaw a file." (LDS Church Historical Department.)

It was with humility and obedience that 120 men accepted a one-year call made by Elder George A. Smith from the pulpit of the Bowery on the Temple Block on a Sunday morning in 1850. Their pioneer assignment was to leave their wives and families and go south to establish an iron mission—"and to be ready in two weeks." (*Ancestry Biography and Family of George A. Smith* [Provo: Brigham Young University Press, 1962], 146.)

These pioneer stories and hundreds more that have touched people's hearts for more than a century are being recast throughout the world today. The circumstances and settings are different. The miles that once took months to cross are now traversed in hours. The names, dates, and challenges have changed but the pioneer spirit is the same.

It was with faith that the first Latter-day Saint meetings in Estipac, Mexico, were held. At first the missionaries and their investigators met in an electrical shop. Water was sprinkled on the dirt floor to keep the dust down, and a fifty-gallon oil drum was rolled to the front to serve as a pulpit. A borrowed white tablecloth was draped over the cardboard box sacrament table. Makeshift, yes, but the first pioneers into the Salt Lake Valley met for Sunday services in the field and leaned against wagon wheels for support. Twenty people came that first week in Estipac, but the next Sunday the electrical shop was closed. Brother Nicolas Gonzalez offered, "You may use my house. I have been building two extra rooms. I don't need the rooms. I don't know why I was building them. But now I know. There is space there for the people." The missionaries knew God had prepared a place for them.

It was with charity that Relief Society sisters, led by their president Iby Subowo, cared for each other in Indonesia in 1976, even though they had little to share. Every morning before they began their cooking, each sister would hold back a spoonful of rice. By Sunday each sister had a small bag of rice to take to the meeting. The sisters would pray to know who needed the rice, and then all would go for the visit. The frontier ethic is one of sharing, not hoarding, however scant the supplies.

It was with courage that Russian Andrei Seminov joined the Church. For years he had been an agnostic. "I had looked for truth," he said, "but when I first heard the Latter-day Saint doctrines I was afraid. The standards seemed too high, too impossible to live. Since then I've learned that there is a source of strength to help me live this way."

It was with patience that members in East Germany and other countries behind the Iron Curtain waited for decades to reestablish Church association. For decades their governments limited and often forbade their meeting and their teaching the gospel to others. In the meantime, the members did what they could. They fasted the third Sunday of every month for the return of the missionaries. When the doors were finally opened, a young missionary, one of the first sent into East Germany, exclaimed, "It was a great honor to be the answer to someone's forty-year-old prayers."

Pioneers. Today they are building Zion in Sweden and South Africa, South Carolina and Peru. Diligent gospel pioneers have always led the way, not just in this dispensation but in earlier ones, too. Moses led his people out of Egypt, and they wandered in the wilderness for forty years before finally reaching the promised land. Lehi and his family faced countless unknowns in their journey to their promised land. And the apostle Peter leaped over the side of the Galilean fishing boat to begin his pioneering in the Church by walking on water. Their experiences and those of the pioneers who crossed the plains of North America in the mid-1800s remind us that the most critical journey of all is to come unto Christ. Pioneers—may we be in their company.

*I will take you one of a city, and two of a family,*
*and I will bring you to Zion.*
Jeremiah 3:14

# FAITH AND HOPE

Leaving Nauvoo in the winter of 1845, the Saints faced severe weather and untamed countryside as they crossed Iowa heading west. More than a thousand pioneers lost their lives at this early stage of the trek. Caught up in the drama of the experience, William Clayton wrote new words for a traditional English tune. He recorded in his journal, "This morning I composed a new song, 'All is Well.'" Later titled "Come, Come Ye Saints," it was often sung at evening campfires on the plains and has become a hallmark of the pioneer tradition in the Church.

Brother Clayton knew the hardships of coming to Zion, having supervised more than two hundred Saints on an eleven-week voyage from Liverpool, England. When he arrived in Nauvoo in 1840, he wrote to his family about the trip across the Atlantic:

"We have sometimes almost suffocated with heat . . . sometimes almost froze with cold. We have had to sleep on boards instead of feathers, and on boxes which was worse. We have had our clothes wet through without the privilege of drying them or changing them. We have had to sleep out-of-doors in very severe weather. Don't suppose for a moment that all will be peace and ease. . . . These are days of tribulation and we must endure. . . .

"If you will be faithful you have nothing to fear from the

journey. The Lord will take care of his saints." (10 Dec. 1840, LDS Church Historical Department.)

---

# LIVING THE GOSPEL IN MISTOLAR

On the deserts of Paraguay is the small village of Mistolar. This community is distinct: all the villagers are members of The Church of Jesus Christ of Latter-day Saints.

In the early days of the Church, whole congregations were sometimes converted. Wilford Woodruff's prompting to preach in the south of England is one of the best-known examples of the Lord's leading a missionary to a group of people ready to accept the gospel. Similarly, Paraguayan mission president Merle Bair felt prompted to seek out Walter Flores, a native of the deserts of the Chaco in Paraguay, whom he saw in a television interview. It took three years for the missionaries to find Flores, but once he was taught, he readily accepted the gospel. His testimony of Jesus Christ and of his Church was so compelling that several hundred of his fellow Indians were converted as well.

Wanting to gather away from worldly influences to establish a Zion community, as had the Utah pioneers, these new Saints secured a large stretch of land in the desolate and uninhabited area of Paraguay near the Pilcomayo River, which runs between Mistolar and the northern border of neighboring Argentina. For food, the people planted gardens and fished. Their efforts to become self-sufficient were proving successful.

They were isolated and happy, but, like the pioneers in the American West, these Paraguayan Saints were at the mercy of the elements. As the snows melted in the Andes Mountains, the Pilcomayo River overflowed its banks and flooded the small community. The residents were forced to reestablish their settlement about six miles from the river. But the floods came again, this time with greater force and even higher water. Their tiny chapel, homes, gardens, fences—all were washed away or destroyed. They were left with only the clothes they were wearing when the floods came. For more than a month they waded through knee-deep water.

Yet their faith remained strong.

Elder Ted E. Brewerton of the Seventy and a member of the Area Presidency was sent from Argentina to help. Argentine leaders helped prepare supplies for him to take to the Saints in Mistolar.

The relief supplies filled two small trucks. There was a treadle sewing machine, bolts of fabric, and quantities of rice, beans, and salt. They also tucked in a copy of *Gospel Principles,* recently translated into Nivacle, the dialect of these Indian people.

From Argentina to Mistolar in Paraguay was a hard, two-day trip. The first day the company made good time, traveling nearly three hundred miles on a good road, and arrived in Filadelfia, Paraguay, after seven hours. The next day, they traveled a heavily rutted, sun-baked route. They spent more than nine hours going little more than half the distance traveled the day before. Had there been the slightest rain, the uneven road would have quickly become muddy and impassable.

Elder Brewerton described what they found when they arrived at the village of Mistolar:

"We were warmly welcomed by mostly women and children. I asked where some of the men were and was told they were hunting. When I asked what the men were hunting, the sisters said, 'Anything.'" Some of the men had walked the twelve-mile round trip to the river to fish.

The settlement's surviving livestock were three sheep, a few chickens and goats, and a scrawny dog. That they had little nourishing food or clothing made the 20-degree winter weather of June that much colder. At night, their stick-and-reed homes offered little protection from freezing temperatures.

Their situation was bleak, but smiling villagers greeted the relief team. They had endured extreme hardship for months, and they faced calamity with faith and with no complaints.

That afternoon, the Saints of Mistolar slaughtered one of the remaining sheep to provide their guests a suitable meal. Said Elder Brewerton, "We ate sparingly of the meat, knowing they would use anything we left."

Sympathetic to the circumstances of the people and conscious that the Nivacle Indians are particularly susceptible to disease and early death, Elder Brewerton asked the young president of the Mistolar Branch, "Do you have any sick among your members?"

The young priesthood leader paused, and said, "I don't think so; let me ask the other brethren." A few minutes later he returned. "My brethren told me, 'Of course we have no sick.'" His explanation was simple. "There are thirty-nine of us who hold the Melchizedek Priesthood. We watch over and bless our people."

Elder Brewerton then asked, "Do you have any members who are not quite as active as the rest?" The branch president replied, "Elder Brewerton, of course not. We have accepted the Lord through baptism. We are all true Saints, totally active in our worship of the Lord."

That evening at the branch meeting, a sister offered a prayer Elder Brewerton long remembered: "Father, we have lost our beautiful chapel, we have lost our clothing, we no longer have homes, we have no food to eat, we don't have any materials to build anything, we have to walk ten kilometers to get a drink of dirty river water and don't have a bucket. But we desire to express to thee our gratitude for our good health, for our happiness, and for our Church membership. Father, we want thee to know that under any conditions, we will be true, strong, and faithful to the covenants we made to thee when we were baptized."

The faith and hope of the Saints touched the visitors. Elder Brewerton reported, "During the meeting, we dedicated their land to the Lord. We visited each family's site and saw where they would plant their gardens when the rains would come."

Back in Argentina, Elder Brewerton learned that the rains had not come as the people had anticipated, but the faithful Saints of

Mistolar planted their gardens anyway, and the deep moisture from the floods was enough to start a crop.

Finally the rains did come, producing a rich harvest more than sufficient for their needs. Fishing, too, exceeded the hopes of the people.

The next year, the Andes were packed with snow almost twice the previous year's measure that had caused the grave flooding. Concerned, Elder Brewerton inquired about the Pilcomayo River and the condition of the Saints of Mistolar. "Don't worry," they reported, "we will not be flooded this year because our land was dedicated." Twice the floodwaters surged down the river and flowed over the land but receded before reaching Mistolar.

> *Verily I say unto you, I have not found*
> *so great faith, no, not in Israel.*
> Matthew 8:10

# WHEN I SAY JUMP

Missionaries are often called to labor in their own land. They know the culture, the people, the language. When the pioneers first settled the Salt Lake Valley, missionaries quickly were dispatched to India, to Chile, and to other distant regions of the world. But they were also sent to the Indians nearby, to areas where the missionaries themselves had grown up, and to other Latter-day Saint settlements to colonize and bolster communities.

In 1965 when Sela Feinga and her husband Ha'unga of Tonga were sent to the remote island of Fotuha'a to serve a mission, she was overwhelmed. The young couple had sold all their possessions to finance their mission. For their small home and their farm produce they received thirty-six Tongan dollars. Their five-month-old daughter only added to Sela's fears. The baby was sick; the weather was threatening. Yet the mission president promised as he set Sela apart that though they would encounter extreme hardships, the Lord would be with them and strengthen them if they were faithful.

The trip to the island was difficult. Storms and turbulent seas stretched the first part of the journey to two weeks. The baby developed a high temperature, and Sela too became sick.

As they neared their destination, they heard of the horrors of landing at this island whose rocky cliffs were pounded by the ocean. The seas made mooring a boat impossible. They had to switch from a motor launch to an outrigger canoe and then jump into the ocean, swim to a prominent precipice, and drag themselves onto the ledge and safety.

Those unable to swim had an even more harrowing arrival. The person guiding the outrigger paddled to a rocky ledge jutting out into the ocean and the local people gathered on land to catch any baggage—and any nonswimmers. The transfer required perfect timing. The canoe had to be maneuvered just right so as not to smash into the rocks. The one arriving had to jump at just the right moment or fall to the depths below. Those receiving had to be ready.

Sela couldn't swim. And of course, there was the baby. By now the scattering of little pustules all over her body made it clear that she had the measles. But they were on assignment from the Lord, so Sela and her husband resolved to go on as planned.

She described their arrival at the island: "I wrapped our little one in a blanket and boarded the small open boat that would take us to Fotuha'a. There was no shelter. A light drizzle accompanied us all the way. As we approached the island from a distance, I looked longingly for houses and trees or a friendly sandy beach. Only formidable cliffs and rocky coasts loomed in front of us. We circled the island twice. Apparently our captain wanted to see if another landing spot was better than the usual one. The waves around us were huge. As we contemplated the landing point, I think for the first time I sensed fear in my husband. A few of the island citizens had already begun to congregate on the rocky ledge, waiting to receive us and our goods.

"When the canoe came out to get us, we got into it without incident. It was a small outrigger paddled by a young school-teacher on the island. When we got close to the rock, he said, 'We will count the waves. When one big enough comes in to lift us up even with the top of the ledge, you must jump onto the rock or throw your goods to people standing there. They will give the orders at the precise moment.'

"The rain continued to fall. Ha'unga held our sick baby, still wrapped in her blanket. I was nearly numb with fear. As we got closer to the treacherous landing, the schoolteacher said to my husband, 'Prepare the baby! They will give the orders for her first.'

"The order came to my husband almost instantly from the man on the ledge. 'Hey, you, sir, holding the baby. Take off the blanket and remove all its clothes.'

"'How can that be? The baby is sick with measles. You should not take off her clothes.'"

The paddler spoke sternly to Ha'unga. "You must take off everything, because you are going to have to throw the baby ashore. You can't risk the man dropping it on the rocks or in the ocean because of the blanket or any loose covering."

The command from the ledge came again. "Hurry up. Remove the baby's clothes entirely." But Sela's poor husband simply could not do it. By now he was as terrified as she.

Instantly the young schoolteacher wrenched the baby from Ha'unga's arms. In a second he had removed every stitch of her clothing except her diaper. The voice from the ledge yelled again. "OK, when I say throw, then throw the baby. I'll tell you which is the right wave."

Sela described the tense moments: "In rushed a wave and lifted the canoe but not quite high enough. Down we went out of sight as the ocean retreated. Up again we came on the back of another wave. Not high enough still. Down again out of sight. As we rose on the next wave, I heard the command, 'Throw the baby.' I screamed and then held my breath. I could not bear to see it. The next words were my husband's, 'Worry no more. The baby is safe ashore.'

13

"I had no time to be grateful.

"'You are next, woman,' shouted the man on the ledge.

"How I was to be transported ashore I had no idea, since I couldn't be thrown. 'You will jump at the exact moment I tell you,' he instructed.

"By now I was hysterical with fear. Four times the 'right' wave came, with the schoolteacher expertly maneuvering the canoe close to the ledge and the man commanding me to jump. I could not do it. I simply clung to my husband trembling. Finally, in anger, the man said, 'Woman, do you want to see your baby again or not? Now when I tell you to jump, jump with all your strength.'

"For a moment then I seemed to have my right mind. I prayed again and said, 'Oh, Lord, please show thy love and help me now for my poor baby's sake.'

"'One, two, three, jump!' shouted the man. With my eyes closed, I jumped as best I could." Her next sensation was that of being pulled up onto the ledge and safety. Her husband followed on the next wave. Their mission had begun.

> *Be strong and of a good courage; be not afraid, neither*
> *be thou dismayed: for the Lord thy God is with thee*
> *whithersoever thou goest.*
> Joshua 1:9

# NO PLACE FOR A TEMPLE

When Latter-day Saint Peter Trebilcock was sixteen years old, he was challenged by his Sunday School teacher to invite his school friends to a Sunday evening fireside. Four came. They watched a film, listened to a speaker, and several participated in subsequent activities. Though they never seriously considered joining the Church, they gained an understanding of its values and teachings. Almost twenty years later, that understanding made a difference for the Church in securing property to build the Preston England Temple.

The first missionaries to England in 1837 began their work in Preston, baptizing the first nine converts in the River Ribble on July 30. More than one hundred fifty years later, when the Church announced plans to build a second temple in England, the area near Preston was a natural choice. Peter Trebilcock, now an architect and the bishop of the Preston Ward, was asked to have his architectural firm design the facility. It was not an easy assignment.

The Area Presidency's office in England was charged with finding a fifteen-acre plot in the northwest of England, because in addition to the temple, the Church intended to build a stake center, a missionary training center, a family history center, a distribution facility, and some housing. After considering three possibilities, property in Chorley, near Preston, was selected.

Officials in the Area Presidency's office negotiated for the tract but were told that the land was zoned for business, not for religious or civic use, and there was no chance that the zoning would be changed. Without a change, no permit could be issued and the Church could not build a temple on this land.

The Area Presidency reported the impasse to President Hinckley, who said, nevertheless, "I feel strongly we should buy the site." Elders Kenneth Johnson and Jeffrey R. Holland reiterated the futility of the situation, and President Hinckley again said, "I want you to buy the site."

The architects were now charged with resolving the zoning issues. They went before the city planning department with pictures of existing temples and a presentation outlining their intentions. "They told us to go away," recalls Brother Trebilcock. "They said, 'We don't want a temple on this site, nice as your temple might be.'" A third time the architects went back, with an even more complete presentation. Again they were told that the master plan for the property called for a business park. Any proposal for a church would be refused.

Bishop Trebilcock returned to President Hinckley with the

news. He expressed his thanks for the opportunity to work on the proposed temple but was resigned to the temple's being built somewhere else. President Hinckley listened to Bishop Trebilcock's analysis of the opposition and then said, "We have every confidence in you."

Bishop Trebilcock went back to work, remembering the promise of President George Q. Cannon at the dedication of the Logan Temple in 1884: "Every foundation stone that is laid for a temple, and every Temple completed . . . lessens the power of Satan on the earth and increases the power of God and Godliness." (*Gospel Truth: Discourses and Writings of George Q. Cannon*, 2 vols. in 1, ed. Jerreld L. Newquist [Salt Lake City: Deseret Book, 1987], 366.)

The Church was committed to the Chorley site.

Bishop Trebilcock and his associates identified all the planning and local council officials involved in the decision making. Then they set up a task force of Church members who knew the people critical to changing the zoning.

Bishop Trebilcock spotted the name of an old school friend on his list. He called him on the telephone. "I'd like to talk to you about the planning issues related to building an LDS temple on the site," said Trebilcock. The two then discussed the other council members, who was in favor, who was against. "They want a business park, an office development," his friend reiterated. "They want jobs, not a church."

Bishop Trebilcock then asked, "How do you feel? Can we count on your support?"

"I know what your church stands for," he replied. Then Brother Trebilcock remembered he was one of the friends who at his invitation had attended that missionary fireside years ago. "And you have my full support," said the council member.

The neighbors near the property were also contacted personally. They, too, were adamantly opposed to the proposed temple. They had already organized into an action group and had produced files "two feet thick" to support the ban on building a temple, recalled Bishop Trebilcock.

The architects advertised a meeting in a local hotel to explain the proposal and ask for neighborhood support. After the formal presentation of the plans, the residents started to ask questions.

"Will there be bells ringing regularly?"

"What about a cemetery?"

When the question was asked, "What goes on inside the temple?" Bishop Trebilcock saw an opportunity for the Spirit to help them. "There are marriages for time and all eternity, and there are baptisms and there is instruction, what we call the endowment," he said. "The temple is a place to contemplate and draw closer to God."

"What about raising funds for the seven proposed buildings?" someone asked. "Will this ambitious building project ever really be finished?"

Bishop Trebilcock reassured them. Church officials had told him and his business associates, none of whom were members of the LDS Church, that "whenever a temple is proposed, the Church puts aside one year in advance all the funds for that project. There is no mortgaging or borrowing. Funds are safe and secure."

"How many Mormon pilgrims would visit the site?"

"We believe this is going to be a busy temple," he responded. "We expect fifty thousand members will visit every year to participate in the holy ordinances."

Then someone called out, "What will the quality of the building be like?" At that point the Spirit prompted Bishop Trebilcock to ask if anyone in the audience had visited a Latter-day Saint temple. A sole hand went up at the back of the room.

"I have visited a Mormon temple," the man volunteered as he stood. "I thought it was lovely. The landscaping was superb. The quality was first class, and the feelings I had when I was there were marvelous." Speaking to his neighbors he urged, "I recommend to you that you support this proposal."

The mood shifted. Soon another man stood who had earlier been an outspoken critic. He said, "I think I speak for everyone in this room when I say we have been most impressed with what we have seen and heard and we want to give you our full support. Now, what can we do to help you?"

When a baffled city council received from that body of citizens a petition bearing scores of names in support of the LDS temple in the town of Chorley, their debate took a proprietary turn. One representative said, "We hear that the temple is going to be called the Preston Temple, but it is going to be in Chorley."

"It doesn't matter what this temple is called," responded another council member. "It will be a landmark for Chorley, it will be good for our town, and we should support it."

By unanimous vote the restrictions were lifted.

*If God had commanded me to do all things I could do*
*them. If he should command me that I should say*
*unto this water, be thou earth, it should be earth;*
*and if I should say it, it would be done.*
1 Nephi 17:50

# WITHOUT THE MOST SIMPLE TOOLS

Elders Larry R. White and Carl Hansen had been in Bangkok, Thailand, less than a month when they began knocking on doors. They had learned a door approach in the Thai language, but beyond that they could not respond to more than two or three basic questions or present discussions. "If we thought that the person we contacted was interested—and our language was such that we weren't always sure—we would take their name and promise to come back when we could speak better," Elder White recalled.

The elders had been transferred from the Southern Far East Mission based in Hong Kong where they had spoken a Chinese dialect based on tones. It was hoped that would provide a base for learning Thai more quickly. They and the four other missionaries had only thirty days of language training at the American

University Alumni School in Thailand before beginning full-time proselyting. Like many early missionaries who went to countries without any knowledge of the language, the elders were working "without the most simple tools." Not only could they not speak the language, but they had no tracts, such as "The Joseph Smith Testimony," no excerpts from the Book of Mormon, and no well-prepared lesson plan to teach those who would listen. Many terms such as *priesthood, church,* and *latter days* did not easily translate into Thai.

The first elder to visit Thailand had been Elam Luddington, who was sent by President Brigham Young in 1853. He was also the last until 1968, when Elders White and Hansen arrived. Elder Luddington had been limited to working with the Europeans in Thailand, and he baptized a ship's captain and his wife before being called home.

On Wednesday, 20 March 1968, Elders White and Hansen were ringing doorbells in a wealthy part of Bangkok. Elder White recalled:

"We came upon an imposing walled-in residence. We could not see through the gate, but shortly after we rang, a servant answered and motioned for us to enter. We explained who we were in Thai, thinking she might change her mind, but she motioned even more vigorously for us to enter."

The two waited at the front door while the maid ran to the back of the house and then returned to let them in. She seated them comfortably in the living room, and in a few moments, "a rather sick looking lady descended from upstairs. She introduced herself in English as Srilaksaana. I felt a need to tell this woman our message," said Elder White, "and I began to tell her in English of the Book of Mormon. I had no sooner begun than the Spirit fell upon me and told me with great force that this lady would join the Church. This manifestation was so forceful that I was overcome by emotion and unable to continue speaking. I passed the book to Elder Hansen to finish the introduction. He did so ably, and we asked for a return appointment. She refused to make a firm appointment but said we could come back any time."

The missionaries returned with a filmstrip, but she showed little interest. She smoked cigarettes during the entire presentation. They returned to teach her a first discussion. Again she was noncommittal and distant. When they taught her about prayer, "she responded that she already prayed to Abraham, Moses, Buddha, Jesus Christ, her ancestors and all great people." The second discussion went worse than the first, but the missionaries were able to sell her an English language Book of Mormon. Had Elder White not had such a profound spiritual witness when they first met, the missionaries would have abandoned further contact.

For another month they met with her and even got her to attend Church services. She brought her daughters and her sister. And then something changed. One day Srilaksaana sat clutching the Book of Mormon when the missionaries arrived. They did not ask and she did not explain what had happened until twenty-five years later. She had been waiting to go out with some of her friends when she noticed the Book of Mormon on the shelf. Because she had paid ten baht (about fifty cents) for it, she felt that she should at least read a little. She casually took the book off the shelf and opened it at random. As soon as her eyes fell upon the first passage, she began to shake, and she felt something which she had never before felt. Immediately, she knew the book was true.

What Srilaksaana realized, in retrospect, was that the Lord had prepared her to receive the gospel since childhood and that she would be instrumental in spreading the gospel message to her fellow Thais.

Born in Bangkok in 1924, Srilaksaana came from a prominent family. Her father was the physician for the royal princes, and her mother was a friend of Her Majesty Queen Intharasksaji. The queen asked to rear six-year-old Srilaksaana in the palace, and her parents agreed.

Srilaksaana lived with the queen until she was seventeen, sleeping in the royal quarters, dining with the queen, and reading to her at night. Srilaksaana became well educated, schooled by European nuns who taught her English and required her to use it in all her class work. Every day she saw the English Bible in her schoolroom and hoped someday to read it. The nuns did not teach religion, however, and she remained faithful to the Buddhist beliefs dominant in her country.

She continued her education at Chulalongkorn University, expanded her language skills, and eventually went to work for a group of high government officials.

But it was The Church of Jesus Christ of Latter-day Saints that really needed her expertise. Two young missionaries without language skills or a Thai translation of the Book of Mormon had been led to her door, and she was able to understand their message. She was prepared for the Church, but she faced obstacles. She had to quit smoking, and she had to tell her decision to the Catholic nuns and priests who had trained her and been her friends for so many years. They did not support her.

Nevertheless, in 1968, on her forty-fourth birthday, Srilak-saana Suntarahut was baptized. In the years that followed she assisted with the translation of the Book of Mormon into Thai and was instrumental in translating the Doctrine and Covenants and the Pearl of Great Price. She served as mission Relief Society president and was a teacher and friend to countless converts. She was always working with someone to instruct them or keep them focused on the truths of the restored gospel.

Said Elder Larry White, who years later returned to Thailand as mission president, "Sister Srilaksaana Suntarahut was a pioneer in her homeland, her help in establishing the Church in Thailand was crucial, and yet a more unlikely convert would be difficult to find. Surely the Church in Thailand would be poorer were it not for her."

> *It shall come to pass . . . that every man shall hear*
> *the fulness of the gospel in his own tongue,*
> *and in his own language.*
> Doctrine and Covenants 90:11

# A BETTER WAY

In 1951 not one Korean national was a member of The Church of Jesus Christ of Latter-day Saints. Forty-five years later, there were four missions in Korea and more than forty-five thousand members. And a temple blessed the lives of the people.

In 1949, when Kim Ho Jik, a well-respected agricultural specialist who directed a Korean agricultural experimentation station, went to America to further his education, he was dedicated to improving the quality of life for his countrymen. In the process he opened the door for the gospel to be preached in his homeland.

Kim understood hunger. Since his youth he had searched for spiritual truths that would fill his soul. He had studied at a Buddhist monastery, investigated the Church of the Heavenly Way, and even joined a Protestant church. But he had never been filled. Perhaps his education kept him looking for doctrines that made sense. The death of one of his sons only increased his desire to learn a better way.

Desiring to learn the latest theories and discoveries in agriculture, he enrolled in a highly competitive and well-regarded graduate program in nutrition at Cornell University in upstate New York. Kim was guided, though he did not know the source. Before he left for America, he felt prompted to sell his home, his cars, and many other possessions, leaving his wife and children with an ample supply of cash to support them while he was gone. When war broke out in Korea in 1950, his obedience to the promptings took on a new dimension. His former home was destroyed by bombs, and all the cars were confiscated by the military. But Kim's family was secure.

While Kim studied at Cornell, he made the rounds of local churches looking for truth. He didn't need to look that far. He shared an office with Oliver Wayman, a doctoral candidate in physiology and, like Kim, an older professional who had returned for additional schooling. Brother Wayman was a Latter-day Saint who lived true to his religion. He didn't smoke, drink, or use vulgar or profane language. He worked long hours but never Sundays. A cheerful man, weaving ideals of optimism and personal integrity into his life, he was happy.

The two men became friends. They discussed many aspects of life—study, education, and international affairs. Religion never came up until one day, as Brother Wayman prepared to leave the office, Kim asked for information about his church.

Brother Wayman gave Kim a copy of *The Articles of Faith,* by Elder James E. Talmage. Kim read it in a week and told his friend he believed it. He next read the Book of Mormon and attested it was the word of God, easier to understand and more complete than the Bible. He hoped to see his Protestant church reform some of its teachings in line with those doctrines. He continued to attend his Protestant meetings, but he visited a local LDS branch.

Everything changed on Brother Wayman's last day at Cornell. As he said his good-byes to his associates, he asked Kim Ho Jik why he had come to the United States. Kim replied that he wanted to improve the knowledge of nutrition in his homeland.

Brother Wayman looked at his friend and bore his testimony that the Lord had brought him to America to receive the gospel and take it home to his people in preparation for missionary work. He added that if Kim stepped aside from that responsibility, the Lord would find another to take his place.

The Church of Jesus Christ of Latter-day Saints took on a new importance in Kim's life. He continued to study, met with the missionaries, and took the discussions. When he was taught the Word of Wisdom, he broke into sobs. "If only I had known all of this when I came here. My government wanted me to find ways to feed our people properly, and without sufficient grazing lands for cattle, we did not know how to do this. My whole time studying in America has been to find ways to feed our people the grains the Lord has always intended for us to use."

He was baptized in the Susquehanna River, the same river in

which Joseph Smith had been baptized 122 years before. When he came up from the water, Brother Kim heard a voice say, "Feed my sheep, feed my sheep." He recorded the experience in the flyleaf of his scriptures with his date of baptism, 29 July 1951: "Words given—feed my sheep."

Brother Kim was the first Korean to join the Church, and when he returned to Korea to his new high government post, his missionary zeal went with him. President Joseph Fielding Smith set him apart as district president in 1955 at the same time his country was dedicated for the preaching of the gospel. For the next three years, while he was vice-minister of education for Korea, President Kim also helped the missionaries in bringing his people to Zion.

His social status and government position contributed directly to establishing the Church in Korea. In 1956 as a member of the Seoul Board of Education, he personally presented the proposal for official government recognition of the Church in Korea. Because of his influence, the proposal was approved. He agreed to act as the financial sponsor and guarantor of the first missionaries into the country.

He honored his sacred responsibilities while serving in his high government post. When Korea's president Syngman Rhee summoned him one Sunday morning, the emissary found President Kim Ho Jik teaching a Sunday School class. Not until he was finished did President Kim leave for the presidential mansion. Meanwhile the president, who was known for fits of anger if kept waiting, waited. When President Kim arrived, President Syngman Rhee demanded an explanation. Calmly, he explained his commitments and priorities: he was teaching a Sunday School class. The president of Korea gazed into Brother Kim's eyes for a long moment and then with resolve said, "You have done well."

President Kim died in 1959. In only eight years he had established, defended, and pioneered Zion in a new land. From his efforts came first-generation members who reared their children in the gospel, read them scriptures, prayed together, and placed value on the Church and its principles. The voice had directed, "Feed my sheep." Brother Kim had found a way.

> *For behold, the Lord doth grant unto all nations, of their*
> *own nation and tongue to teach his word.*
> Alma 29:8

# WHY WOULD I NEED THAT?

When the Soviet bloc broke apart, an imposed lifestyle crumbled with it. Suddenly whole nations of people had choices they had never had before. Marek Vasilkov of Lithuania was one of them.

He first met with the Latter-day Saint missionaries in an apartment in his government housing complex in Vilnius. The elders had a place near his, and he had often seen them on the street. Before long, they were teaching him a second discussion. "I didn't have friends," he recalled. "I had no idea what the future would hold, and I was looking for money to make my life meaningful." So when the missionaries suggested, "Why don't you pray for the Spirit?" he was startled. He wondered, "Why would I need that?"

Much had changed in Lithuania since the break with the Soviet Union. Many people were making money; they could now travel outside the country; they had more opportunities. An economy was growing up around both the industrious and the illegal. Like his peers, Marek wanted some for himself. He wanted a better life than Communism had offered him.

Besides looking for a vocation, he was trying to find meaning and purpose in life. People who had money could buy what they wanted. Was that the answer? People who had intellect could develop expertise to advance themselves. He tried carpentry work but didn't like it. Was education the way to go? He kept asking himself, What is the combination for happiness, for the good life? Money, influence, intellect? Where could he find the answers?

He tried to become a member of a gang whose ties to organized crime appeared to have great influence. Then the leader of the gang was murdered. Another leader was blown up in his car. Not only did these incidents seem senseless but he found that something inside him prevented his joining in any kind of violent or illegal activity.

He next turned to athletics and body building, pursuing a rigorous weight-training program. But the intense effort didn't fill the void he felt. He tried boxing but soon lost interest. He went with a friend on a holiday to the seashore; he found no camaraderie or pleasure in the smoking and drinking that dominated their social activity.

For a time he kept company with a young woman whose family had all the trappings of the new material success. They could buy anything they wanted, yet, to Marek, they didn't seem happy. In fact, they bickered all the time. Their home life reminded him of his own because he was always having arguments with his mother. This was not the lifestyle he was seeking.

At one point he even thought of becoming a monk, although the one thing he wasn't looking for was religion. He had attended the Catholic church a couple of times with his grandmother when he was ten. "I didn't feel a need to go again," he recalled. His grandmother believed and enjoyed the traditions of her faith, but he viewed religion as an exercise for old people. It was not for him. So when his neighbor agreed to meet with Latter-day Saint missionaries and asked Marek to come along, he went grudgingly, as a favor to his neighbor.

The missionary effort in Lithuania had started on the clear spring day of 20 May 1993 with twenty-seven Latter-day Saints gathered on a prominent hill overlooking the city of Vilnius. Said Elder M. Russell Ballard of the Quorum of the Twelve: "From this small beginning, you will see the Church grow and prosper here. There will be many branches and then a district and, in the Lord's due time, there will be stakes. Who knows, if we could look out fifty years, perhaps a small temple. That all depends on us, really, and how diligent we are willing to be, and how wise and prudent we are willing to be as we proceed to establish the kingdom of God in Lithuania.

"The people of this land have a goodness, and many of them have righteousness in their hearts. Let that be touched by the missionaries," prayed Elder Ballard.

In the next six months the missionaries began teaching and baptizing, bringing one of a city, two of a family to Zion. Marek was one of their early investigators.

It was only from a desire to be polite that he agreed to meet for a second discussion. "I didn't like the first one," he admitted honestly. "I was looking for something but not what they offered. I didn't want to get converted to Christianity." His neighbor had declined to return, but Marek was studying English and was interested in the language of the missionaries, if not in their beliefs. After all, he explained, "They lived in a neighboring building, and I could use some friends."

At the second visit, the missionaries talked to him about the Spirit. When Marek asked what it was, "They told me to pray, and God would give me the Spirit."

What happened the next week changed his life. He said: "I was standing in a line in a store, and I noticed an old lady. She pointed to a loaf of bread and asked the clerk how much it cost. It was obvious she couldn't afford to buy it. I thought to myself that I could help her; she needed fifty cents. I gave her the money, and right then something happened. It was like tingles. My skin became loose, and I felt a brilliance inside me I had never felt before. I thought of the missionaries and what they had said about the Spirit. I thought, This is the Spirit. I wanted to jump up high right there in the store. I realized that it was true. It was all true. Everything they said was true. And I had felt the Spirit.

"I went a few yards and immediately the temptations came. Thoughts came that said maybe I didn't feel the Spirit. Maybe I am just confused. But when I told the missionaries of the experience, they assured me that what I had felt was the Spirit. I have learned that every time you feel the Spirit, you are reminded that there is a God."

Baptized on 16 October 1993, Marek Vasilkov, age twenty, became the eighteenth member of the Vilnius Branch of The Church of Jesus Christ of Latter-day Saints. "Can I go on a mission?" he asked the elders shortly after his baptism. The Lord called him less than two years later to serve in the Salt Lake City Utah North Mission. He entered the Mission Training Center in Provo on 30 November 1994.

Said one of his companions, Elder Duncan Calder from Victoria, Canada, who served with him, "Elder Vasilkov has taught me to understand Helaman 15:6:

"'Yea, I say unto you, that . . . they are striving with unwearied diligence that they may bring the remainder of their brethren to the knowledge of the truth; therefore there are many who do add to their numbers daily.'

"Every time we ride our bikes up a hill, I see him in front of me with unwearied diligence, so happy in the work, so willing to do whatever he has to so that the word of the Lord can be spread, and I know I can do it, too."

> *There is a spirit in man: and the inspiration of the*
> *Almighty giveth them understanding.*
> Job 32:8

# TAKING THE GOSPEL HOME

The missionaries first contacted Horacio Tulio Insignares about the gospel in 1968. He was polite but not interested. He wasn't looking for religion. Eight years later he noticed a similar-looking pair of young men getting off a bus. He felt drawn to them and prompted to ask about their church. He, his wife, and two of his children were baptized a month later.

A few years later, while serving as a district president in

Colombia, he again felt a prompting from the Spirit—this time to take the gospel to the community where he lived as a youth. He asked the mission president if elders could be sent to Barrancabermeja, a town about two and a half hours from where he now lived. The mission president reluctantly agreed to send one missionary on a fact-finding visit with the earnest President Insignares. They were to return with a recommendation.

In advance of their visit, Horacio contacted his mother, who was not a Latter-day Saint, and proposed a meeting in her home for family and neighbors to hear his message of the restored gospel. She was interested. When he set out for Barrancabermeja with his wife Dora, their eldest son, and the young missionary, he was excited about the prospects of preaching to so many familiar faces. His mother expected thirty-five people for the meeting.

They were nearing the town when the car broke down. President Insignares remained calm, undaunted by the calamity. "Satan isn't going to stop us," he said. He hid his car in a field, anticipating that it might be stolen while they were gone. Then he hailed a passing bus. When the four of them arrived in town, they went to the scheduled missionary meeting. "Here are the people," he said to the elder. "Teach them while I go get my car."

The Spirit took over.

The missionary fielded questions from the investigators and taught them the gospel. He was convinced that the time was right to open the area and scheduled another meeting. The mission president sent two elders for a day, then for two days, and then for a week. President Insignares arranged for discussions to be held in his mother's home, and he willingly drove the elders back and forth for the meetings.

The people of Barrancabereja had been so much like family to him while he was growing up that now he wanted above all else to help them learn the truths of the gospel of Jesus Christ. It wasn't long before the mission president assigned elders to work full time in Barrancabermeja.

Baptisms came quickly. First was one of President Insignares's relatives and her fiancé. Others followed almost immediately; people were baptized by the dozens. Within a year the branch grew into a ward and just kept growing. After three years there were six hundred members in Barrancabermeja. One ward became two, and the conversions continued.

So did the promptings of the Spirit.

One Sunday President Insignares suddenly felt impressed to go back to Barrancabermeja. He set his other commitments aside and arrived at the church just in time to see an old childhood friend walk in.

The man, too, recognized his friend from his youth, and exclaimed to President Insignares, "I told my wife I would go with her to church today, and if I found a friend there, I would be baptized."

President Insignares smiled. The Lord had wanted him in that meeting. The Lord knew he would stand as a witness of God. His friend was baptized, and not long after he was called as bishop of one of the Barrancabermeja wards.

> *For behold, again I say unto you that if ye will enter in*
> *by the way, and receive the Holy Ghost, it will show*
> *unto you all things what ye should do.*
> 2 Nephi 32:5

# SEVEN TIMES THE NOTE SAID YES

Those who have lived in Bulgaria speak of the stunning countryside, the grand Balkan Mountains, and the choice resorts edging the Black Sea. Picturesque though it is, however, the dramatic scenery did not make bearable the oppressive social and political conditions imposed by the Communist government. Bulgarians feared the government, their associates, and even their "friends." Yet getting out of the country was virtually impossible. To do so would take a miracle.

Kiril and Nevenka Kiriakov, a young dental technician and his wife, had long been praying for a way to leave Bulgaria to rear their children in freedom. A slim chance came in 1963 when Algeria became independent of France. The new country approached the Bulgarian government for assistance in restructuring its economy. The state laboratory was asked to furnish one dental technician for a two-year assignment. Kiril, like each of his six colleagues, hoped to be chosen. He later wrote in his personal history, "My chances were not good. Most of my colleagues had a contact or a relative who held a high position in the government, someone they could rely on for help. I knew of no one who could help me, so I put my entire faith and hope in our Heavenly Father. My wife and I decided that only our fervent prayers to the Lord could open the door to the free world."

Everyone at the lab recognized that the position in Algeria was a passport to freedom. When the day of the selection came, "one of my colleagues proposed that we decide the matter by drawing lots, placing seven folded pieces of paper in a hat, six of which would have no written on them and one would contain the word yes."

This seemed fair, and all agreed. The slips of paper were prepared and placed in the hat. Kiril drew his and opened it. "I could not believe my eyes," he said, "the piece of paper I had drawn had yes written on it."

Immediately his associates protested the outcome because he had been in the laboratory only eight months, and many of them had worked there for a lifetime. They insisted on another drawing. A second time Kiril drew the yes. Again they refused to accept the results. He returned the slip and drew another time but with the same astonishing result. Four more times the group drew from the hat. Each time, Kiril opened his slip of paper to find the yes. Finally, instead of objecting, the amazed group gathered around him. Although the Bulgarian government had outlawed all religious conviction, his associates agreed that the only way he could have drawn the yes slip seven times in a row was with the help of God. They had witnessed a miracle.

The Kiriakov family spent the next two years in Algeria. For them it was "like living in paradise." At the end of their assignment, when Kiril was expected to return with his family to Bulgaria, he petitioned his government to return by way of France. Usually the procedure was to force the family to return separately to limit the possibility of defection. Kiril recalled, "The idea presented itself to add the words 'and family' on my exit permit and we were successful in obtaining tourist visas to France for the entire family." The Kiriakovs defected in France.

Fifteen days later a bloody coup d'etat toppled the Communist government in Algeria, and all Bulgarians were rounded up and flown home en masse. But the Kiriakov family was safe in Marseilles.

About two years later, this Bulgarian family learned the reason the Lord had said yes to their leaving their homeland. Two missionaries of The Church of Jesus Christ of Latter-day Saints knocked on their door, "something that never would have happened in Bulgaria." The Lord had opened the way for them to come to Zion.

*In their affliction they will seek me early.*
Hosea 5:15

# ALMOST WORD FOR WORD

Doors open for the Church in foreign lands one at a time. And usually the people embrace the gospel only a few at a time—one of a city, two of a family. It has always been so.

But once these pioneer seeds are planted, the gospel begins to grow—just as it did in the early days in England and other European countries—and produces a great gathering of people. This pattern can still be seen around the world.

Said Elder George I. Cannon, a General Authority assigned to the Philippines area two decades ago, "It really seems to be the time for the Filipino people to receive the gospel."

He was right.

On 28 May 1961 Elder Gordon B. Hinckley gathered a small group of Latter-day Saints at the American War Memorial Cemetery on the outskirts of Manila. He said, "What we begin here will affect the lives of thousands and thousands of people in this island republic, and its effect will go from generation to generation for great and everlasting good." Four elders officially opened missionary work, and through the doors of the gospel of Jesus Christ came thousands of people. Within a year, there were 250 members. By 1965, 1,350 people had joined the Church.

Those early pioneers were dedicated. In the 1975 Philippine Area Conference, Latter-day Saints gathered to listen to President Spencer W. Kimball. One sister, Lourdes Gomez, attended the meetings to feel the Spirit and be in the presence of a prophet of God. She had sacrificed to be there, and she came with "ears to hear." As President Kimball spoke she committed to memory his burning testimony, his words of love and devotion to the Lord's work. To her husband's amazement, she could quote the message from the prophet almost word for word. But there had been no interpreter at the session, and Sister Gomez did not speak or understand English. Still she heard and understood all that was said. She insisted President Kimball had spoken in Tagalog. Her husband insisted he had spoken in English. English it was. But Sister Gomez had heard the message in Tagalog.

Her "ears to hear" and understand the words of the prophet typified the strength of the Church among the Filipinos. At last the construction of a temple was announced at general conference on 4 April 1981. The people of the Philippines, like the pioneers in St. George and Logan, Utah, immediately began to sacrifice to build their temple. President Gordon B. Hinckley paid tribute to their efforts in his prayer at the dedication of the Manila Temple:

"This nation of the Philippines is a nation of many islands whose people love freedom and truth, whose hearts are sensitive to the testimony of thy servants, and who are responsible to the message of the eternal gospel. We thank thee for their faith. We thank thee for their spirit of sacrifice. We thank thee for the miracle of the progress of thy work in this land. In a few short years it has grown from small beginnings to its present stature with many established stakes of Zion." (*Church News,* 30 Sept. 1984, 5–10.)

Local leader Ruben M. Lacanienta related the Old Testament story of the destruction of a wicked city that could have been saved if the Lord could have found ten righteous persons living there. That the city was ultimately wiped off the face of the earth indicated that not even ten righteous persons could be found among the thousands and thousands of its inhabitants.

"The presence of the Manila Temple of The Church of Jesus Christ of Latter-day Saints in this country at this time is an assurance that out of its portals will come not only ten but hundreds, even thousands of righteous Latter-day Saints that will act as a catalyst for righteousness among the fifty million Filipinos in this country."

> *To every thing there is a season, and a time*
> *to every purpose under the heaven.*
> Ecclesiastes 3:1

# WONDERFUL! WONDERFUL!

As a little boy, Daeyoon Kim was one of those children, so common in Korea, who spent his days following the missionaries everywhere. The elders lived near his home in Chinhae, so he pestered them for treats, games, talk, attention. They were always kind. How could he not like them? After a while, he started following them to church. When he was twelve, some missionaries went beyond conversation and teasing and taught him the discussions. He was baptized. Because of the warmth and generous nature of the elders, he continued to be active.

Several years later, shortly after Daeyoon turned fourteen, the first all-Korea Church conference was announced. The prophet, President Spencer W. Kimball, was traveling from America to speak. The meetings were to be held in Seoul, the nation's capital. Daeyoon wanted to go, but his nonmember parents were troubled about the seven-hour bus ride from Chinhae to Seoul. Because he had relatives in Seoul, his parents finally relented, arranging for Daeyoon to stay with family in the city.

When the day for the conference came, Daeyoon was thrilled as he listened to President Kimball and the other General Authorities. But his seat was at the back of the auditorium, so he could hear the Brethren better than he could see them. He was disappointed to be so near and yet so far. With the innocent faith of youth, he bowed his head and prayed that some day he would be able to personally meet President Kimball and other General Authorities.

The next morning he boarded a bus for the lengthy ride back home. At one point, the bus made a stop to refuel, and Daeyoon got off to buy an ice cream cone in the nearby restaurant. As he walked back to the bus, he noticed an American car with a bumper sticker that read "Families are Forever." With melting ice cream dripping from the cone, he ran back to the restaurant, hoping to meet some American Mormons.

Suddenly his heart stopped. His prayer of the day before was to be answered not years from now, but today! There, across the room, stood President Kimball. Full of confidence from his positive experiences with many missionaries, Daeyoon rushed across the room, thrust out his hand, and introduced himself in simple English. "Hi! I'm Daeyoon Kim. I'm a Mormon."

President Kimball enthusiastically grasped Daeyoon's small, sticky hand and invited him to sit at his table. President Kimball pulled out his handkerchief and, smiling, wiped the ice cream off the boy's face. "Are your parents Mormons?" he asked.

"No," the boy replied with a downward glance. "Good!" was the prophet's immediate response. "You can help convert them. Where are you from, Brother Kim?"

"Chinhae, seven hours southeast of Seoul. I've just been to the conference to hear you speak."

"I'm proud of you for your devotion in traveling such a

distance," said President Kimball. "I'd like you to meet my wife and the General Authorities traveling with us." And he formally introduced Daeyoon to the other visitors.

Very soon the bus was ready to leave, and Daeyoon had to say good-bye. President Kimball again took the youth by the hand, looked him in the eye, and said, "The Church needs you to build the kingdom in Korea, Brother Kim. Will you serve a mission? Will you help build the kingdom of God?" With fervor, Daeyoon promised he would.

President Kimball put his arms around the young man, hugged him close, and whispered in his ear, "Wonderful! Wonderful! Wonderful!"

*Ask, and it shall be given you.*
Matthew 7:7

# A SMALL FAVOR

When ear, nose, and throat surgeon Gedeon Kereszti watched a documentary about The Church of Jesus Christ of Latter-day Saints on Hungarian national television, he was intrigued with the beliefs. Most appealing was the concept that families could be together in the eternities. A religion including that premise was what the Keresztis very much wanted. But Hungary, a country under Communist control, had been closed to religious teachings for decades.

On the other side of the world, in Salt Lake City, Utah, the family of Kim Davis, also an ear, nose, and throat specialist, had been praying to find a family to introduce to the gospel. They had set a goal to find a family within six months.

This was not unusual for the Davis family. The six Davis children and their parents had been acquainting people with the gospel for years during the time they had lived in Boston and Washington, D.C. Now, settled in Salt Lake City, they had fasted and prayed, but so far they had found no one. Their six months had almost passed.

Then Dr. Davis got a letter from a physician in Hungary. The return address was no surprise to him because he had written several articles for international medical journals detailing his research and findings. Professionals from foreign countries often corresponded with him about his research. But this letter was more than a query for information: it was an answer to prayer.

Dr. Kereszti in Ajka, Hungary, wrote asking for more information about a church he had seen profiled on television—The Church of Jesus Christ of Latter-day Saints, based in Salt Lake City, Utah, USA. He and his son had pored over medical journals until they found an address in Utah. It belonged to Dr. Kim Davis. Their request was simple: Would the doctor forward his letter to some information center that could supply him with material about this church?

The Davis family headed for the Church Distribution Center and scooped up pictures and other materials about the Church. They packed a box for their new investigator family. They wrote their testimonies, copied a family picture, and sent everything off with the official materials.

No doubt the Keresztis had hoped for some sort of information packet. They got much more. They got a personal witness from each member of the Davis family. The testimonies borne by the children and the parents spoke of their love for the gospel and their love for each other.

The two families began exchanging letters and pictures, and the Davises contacted the president of the Vienna Austria East Mission, whose area of responsibility included Hungary.

In February 1986 the mission president met with the Keresztis to teach them the gospel, answer their questions, and broaden their understanding. Later that month the three were baptized in Vienna. A picture taken at the event was sent straight to the Davises.

Their baptism was just a beginning. Dr. Kereszti pioneered establishing the Church in Hungary. One year later, in April 1987,

Elder Russell M. Nelson of the Quorum of the Twelve dedicated Hungary for the preaching of the gospel. Missionary work began officially in June 1988 when legal recognition was granted to the Church. On June 24, Elder Nelson, representing the Church, received that formal declaration in Budapest. He was accompanied by Elder Hans B. Ringger of the First Quorum of the Seventy, Dennis B. Neuenschwander, president of the Austria Vienna East Mission, Dr. Gedeon Kereszti, president of the Hungarian District, and his counselor Dr. Peter Paul Vargas.

*I shall lengthen out mine arm unto them.*
2 Nephi 28:32

# "I HAVE ONLY ONE WISHES"

When Stanley and Mavis Steadman and James and Helen Bateman arrived in Hanoi, Vietnam, in 1993 as English teachers from The Church of Jesus Christ of Latter-day Saints, they were entering what they learned to call "the promised land."

The Vietnamese were curious about these teachers. Their arrival was announced in the press and on national television. In a few short months the results they were having were so impressive that the Communist government asked the Church to send more couples, even offering to provide their housing and other expenses. Today the Traditional Hall, a memorial in Hanoi, features a display dedicated to the Church and the service given by its members.

The Steadmans and Batemans opened the door to the gospel through service. Hanoi was so different from their homes in America or from Australia where the four had served together as missionaries. Yet they worked at feeling at home. They lived on rice and vegetables and hung their clothes on a line strung from the rooftop of their apartment building. The sisters cut each other's hair, though Stan once, just once, made the mistake of getting his hair cut by the barbers on the street for a dollar. Not only was his haircut peculiar but, Sister Steadman reported, "Our doctor friends said he paid too much—should have been only thirty cents."

Their reports home showed how quickly they became at ease in the country. "What boggled our minds the first week or so is now commonplace: the women, barefoot and selling their produce in huge baskets hanging from a bamboo pole balanced on their shoulders; or buying a loaf of bread from an old black-toothed woman who squats all day in front of our apartment.

"The streets are filled with hundreds of bicycles. There are no cars, and our biggest challenge is to cross safely. . . . The homes are humble. A plastic surgeon makes forty dollars a month. A teacher makes fourteen dollars. These people are choice spirits of God, and their day will come."

The Steadmans and the Batemans had come to teach English and to open doors for the Church. They found eager students. Soon there was a waiting list to get into their classes. Sister Steadman related: "We are teaching 160 children at the school and 200 doctors, ministers of the Cabinet, engineers, and selected teachers from all the schools and University of Hanoi. We were promised only 20 students to a class. We have more than 40. They are hanging out the windows, sitting in the halls, on the floor, and crowded together with five on a bench that only holds three.

"At the school where we teach the children (ages seven to thirteen), the door to the street is always open, and there is always a crowd of onlookers, children, parents, other teachers, and just curious passersby. There are usually even more outside than inside our crowded rooms."

The setting was not exactly ideal, but they improvised: "The classrooms are stark and bare with the benches in regimented rows." The first thing Sister Steadman did was rearrange them into a more informal seating. The first thing the kids did was put them back the way they were. It was hard to break with tradition.

The teachers had no teaching materials—colored paper and

other supplies did not exist. They made bulletin boards out of the cardboard boxes their own belongings came in and decorated them with packing material. Sister Steadman wrote, "This will be a struggle, but I am learning what a privilege it is to sacrifice."

They put up a sign in the classroom announcing "ONLY EN-GLISH WILL BE TAUGHT IN THIS ROOM." Said Sister Steadman, "We have no interpreter—just the Lord!"

Although at first they were not allowed to speak of the Church or invite anyone to their meetings, their mission began with a "thrilling experience." Sister Steadman recorded: "The four of us held the first sacrament meeting ever in Hanoi, Vietnam. We bought a small silver tea set, a loaf of bread from a woman on the street, boiled water, and covered all with a white lace handkerchief. We felt the ceiling open and the glory of the Lord pour out upon us."

That glory quickly became apparent in their work.

They always began the children's class with a song. Wrote Sister Steadman: "Stan teaches them a new one every day. They sing with all their hearts and souls. They are so innocent. I accompany them on a keyboard we brought with us. Can you imagine the thrill we had when Stan taught them 'Give Said the Little Stream'? They just belted it out with unbounded enthusiasm. I couldn't even play because the tears were streaming down my face."

Not everything the Steadmans and Batemans did was in the classroom or one-on-one. They planned a bold cultural event for the community, miraculously presenting Handel's *Messiah,* complete with orchestra and chorus. The performers received standing ovations for their professional performances, and the image of the Church was enhanced by the production.

Every day Sister Steadman identified a "courage-to-go-on incident," pioneering moments like those of the early Saints who, too, had left their homes to build the kingdom of God in a foreign land. She writes of the first: "Yesterday a woman doctor stopped me after class. She had a gift in her hand and she said, 'I buy this at Laos-China border. I like you, Mrs. Mavis. I like you teach. I like you dress. I like you have this.' She gave me a small bone-carved fan. I cried. It will be one of my treasures."

The second clearly reflected the influence these first missionaries had as they shared the Spirit of the Lord in their teaching assignment: "Two days ago I read a fairy tale called 'Three Wishes' to the classes and followed it up for conversation practice by asking each one to give their three wishes if they could have them. One dear old doctor, still in the square white cap and white operating gown that they come to class in, said, 'I have only one wishes. I wish you be Vietnamese so you stay with us alway.'

"We love these dear people," wrote Sister Steadman to her friends at home. "They will be ready when the time comes for the missionaries. This whole country will be."

> *Hope for a better world . . . which*
> *hope cometh of faith.*
> Ether 12:4

# COURAGE AND DILIGENCE

In May 1848 nearly two thousand Saints were making ready for their journey across the plains. "Every exertion," wrote a member of the company, "is making to go West."

Nearing the end of the trail, these wearied pioneers encountered the roughest going of all. The year before, in the vanguard journey, Orson Pratt had written that near the end of the journey "the country exhibited a broken succession of hills piled on hills, and mountains on mountains in every direction." They were the last barriers to Zion.

When the company arrived in the Salt Lake Valley, pioneer Hosea Stout wrote of a welcome but grueling victory over time and conditions: "Thus ends this long and tedious journey from the land of our enemies, & I feel free and happy that I have escaped from their midst. But there is many a desolate & sandy plain to cross. Many a rugged sage bed to break through. Many a hill and hollow to tug over and many a mountain to pass. And many frosty nights to endure in mid-summer."

With courage and diligence, modern-day pioneers face "hills piled on hills," "desolate plains," and "frosty nights in mid-summer." (Juanita Brooks, *On the Mormon Frontier: The Diary of Hosea Stout* [Salt Lake City: Utah State Historical Society, 1964], 1:327; entry for 24 Sept. 1848.)

# I'LL TAKE CARE OF THIS

The plane rushed David Horne from Armenia to France. Meanwhile industrialist Jon M. Huntsman in Salt Lake City collected a team of burn specialists from the University of Utah hospital and flew with them in his private jet to France to rescue his friend. The day before, on 14 January 1996, a freak propane explosion at his apartment in Yerevan had burned Brother Horne over more than 85 percent of his body. When Jon reached France, his severely injured friend, struggling to speak, looked up at the face he knew so well and said, "Go home, Jon. I'll take care of this." Then he passed out. He died three days later.

David Horne spent the last six years of his life helping the people of Armenia. What began as an effort to help rebuild this Soviet satellite after a devastating earthquake in December 1988 became the primary focus of Brother Horne's life.

Jon Huntsman had brought him into the effort to improve construction techniques and upgrade materials to rebuild Armenian homes and businesses. Brother Horne, as director of Armenian Projects for Huntsman Chemical Company, supervised building a cement plant to provide building supplies for the people.

In the course of his work, David Horne made many friends for the Church in the community; indeed, the Armenians knew him as their friend. When news of his accident spread through the town, the streets to the airport were lined with hundreds whose lives had been changed by him. At his funeral service, letters of tribute were presented from friends and business and government leaders in Armenia.

What had taken this successful building contractor from his Salt Lake City home to a foreign country halfway around the world? He had responded to a mission call from the Church to donate his time and skills to help build safe homes for earthquake victims. He was to supervise the construction of a precast concrete fabrication plant that would produce enough units to build 6,500 apartments and provide housing for 25,000 people annually. The plant was dedicated in Yerevan, Armenia, on 24 June 1991.

At that time, in gratitude for the relief efforts extended to the Armenian people by the Church and such individuals as Brother Horne and philanthropist Jon Huntsman and his family, the Republic of Armenia donated land to the Church for a building in the capital city of Yerevan. The four-story, marble-faced, multipurpose building would be used as a meetinghouse, offices, and residences for Church volunteers assisting in managing the concrete plant operated jointly by Huntsman Chemical and the Armenian government. Elder Russell M. Nelson, in accepting the gift of land, pledged "to use the building on this site to teach of the Fatherhood of God and the brotherhood of man."

David Horne had done just that.

As a dedicated Church leader, he helped establish a branch of the Church that expanded under his guidance to 450 members. Missionaries were called from the Armenian branch to serve in parts of Russia. Brother Horne's wife, Jeanne, who joined him as a Church humanitarian service missionary for three years, helped translate the hymnbook into Armenian. His last service to Armenia was to distribute hundreds of pairs of eyeglasses he had collected in the United States for the people in Armenia.

On 24 June 1991, in his prayer dedicating Armenia for the preaching of the gospel, Elder Dallin H. Oaks petitioned that the land's inhabitants, as they tried to overcome the difficulties of the past and go forward, might realize "the benefit of their righteous labors" and feel the "cool breeze of freedom." As a pioneer building Zion in another land, David Horne had given that "righteous labor" and had helped sound "the song of liberty, the song of freedom."

> *But charity is the pure love of Christ, and it endureth*
> *forever; and whoso is found possessed of it*
> *at the last day, it shall be well with him.*
> Moroni 7:47

# INSIDE THE FRONT COVER

When ward mission leader Victor Brown donated a copy of the Book of Mormon to the public library in Hamilton, Ontario, Canada, it was an act of faith. He hoped that people would read the book and be converted. Three times he returned to the library to update his address and phone number on the sheet he had carefully placed in the front with the bold notation, "For more information." That was thirty years before, and not one person had called.

And then Kenneth Evans, seeking to find truths about life and death, checked out the Book of Mormon from the Hamilton library. He read it that night and all the next day. He called Victor Brown.

Kenneth and his wife had been sincerely searching for several years. His daughter recalls: "They had attended neighborhood churches, Bible seminars, and engaged in earnest prayer. I would sometimes awaken from my sleep to see my dad praying. I asked him once what he was praying about and he said, 'I'm praying that I can somehow teach you kids the right things about God, but I'm not sure what those things are yet.'"

Two years into their quest, "my mom answered the door and found two well-dressed young men standing there. She'd had a lot of door-to-door salesmen lately. As soon as one of the young men began to speak of a certain church with a long name she quickly said, 'We have our own church, thank you,' and shut the door."

But when their minister announced a new policy of meeting an hour earlier to give families more time for recreation on Sunday, the Evanses felt it was time to look in earnest for another church. They wanted greater spirituality and truth, not more time for recreation on Sunday.

Kenneth had always been interested in the ancient ruins of Mexico and Central and South America. He and an associate at work, Ray, had often talked of the mysteries and splendor of those civilizations. Ray mentioned that while he had been living in England, he had heard from two young men in a series of discussions the unbelievable story of a young man named Joseph Smith who had dug up a book about the ancient ruins and the societies that had built them. The missionaries had not interested Ray in the Church, but he did remember that the book was called the Book of Mormon.

That week the Evans family visited the public library, where Kenneth searched the files for the Book of Mormon. It was not listed. But by looking for works relating to "Mormons," he found *What of the Mormons?* by Gordon B. Hinckley, and he checked it out. He read the book that night and announced to his family, "This sounds like just the church we've been looking for! Now, we need to find a Book of Mormon."

They checked with the local bookstore only to be told rather curtly that they carried no such book. That Saturday Kenneth called the main public library downtown and asked the clerk to check the listings for a copy of the Book of Mormon. There was one. Kenneth asked her to hold it for him; he'd be right there.

He and his wife read the book all day and into the evening. They were interested in all they read. Maybe this was what they were seeking!

Inside the front cover of the book, a typed page fastened there by a Victor Brown gave a date thirty years old. In case more information was desired, Victor Brown had returned to the library to change his address and telephone number after each of three moves over the years. But he had moved a fourth time, and he hadn't made it back to make that change.

When Kenneth tried calling the last number listed, he found no one there by the name of Brown. The phone book listed several pages of Browns but no Victor and only one with the initial "V"—a V.E.F. Brown.

He called.

Kenneth abruptly opened the conversation with, "I'd like you to tell me more about your church." Victor Brown thought someone, maybe another ward member, was playing a practical joke. But when Kenneth mentioned the book in the library, Brother Brown recognized the questioner was absolutely sincere.

"I know it's true. I know it's true," Brother Brown answered his caller in a voice full of emotion. Alice Brown, overhearing her husband's conversation, whispered to him, "Invite them to the Missionary Open House this Saturday."

The Evans family came. Many people were milling about between the booths and exhibits, watching the filmstrips and talking in groups. Kenneth and his family felt inconspicuous and comfortable among so many people who, too, showed interest. The Evanses didn't know they were the only investigators in attendance. And their hearts were touched. Their youngest son pleaded with his parents to come back to this place that felt so good.

The elders began visiting their home and teaching them the discussions. Friends, including their former pastor, cautioned them about involvement with the Mormons. But to no avail. On Christmas night, 1967, the Evans family was baptized. "What better way to honor him on this day when we celebrate his birth," their daughter Christine wrote of that poignant memory.

And in gratitude she added, "I often think of Brother Brown, who found his calling as a district missionary challenging but who followed a prompting of the Spirit to place that Book of Mormon in the library, where it waited all those years to be discovered. I think, too, of the missionaries in England, many years ago, who must have spent long hours teaching Ray all those discussions and of how discouraged they must have been when he still rejected their message. Yet he retained just enough knowledge of the Book of Mormon to be the spark my father needed to find out more."

*Thus saith the Lord God; Behold, I, even I, will both*
*search my sheep, and seek them out . . . and will*
*deliver them out of all places where they have*
*been scattered in the cloudy and dark day.*
Ezekiel 34:11–12

# NINE IN THE CAR

At nearly midnight on 16 July 1990, a small, four-passenger Toyota Corolla pulled up in front of the mission home in Freetown, Sierra Leone, West Africa. Nine young elders crawled out of the car and wakened their mission president, Miles Cunningham. The last leg of their harrowing escape from war-torn Monrovia, Liberia, had taken thirty-four hours. They were hungry, stiff, shaken, and exhausted, but they were alive.

Civil war had been raging for six months. Rebels wanted to unseat the president, Samuel Kenyo Doe, who ten years earlier had seized power in a similar war. Tribes had taken sides, and hostilities raged everywhere.

President Cunningham had left Monrovia several months before when the fighting reached the city's borders. The couple missionaries had left with the president.

Before the president departed, he told the remaining elders, who were local missionaries, to stop proselyting, remove their missionary name badges, stay in their quarters, and, if the fighting continued, return to their homes. He left money, food, and a car with the branch counselor.

The fighting intensified. The airport was seized, and water, electricity, and telephones were cut off. The elders were on their own. Lodged in different parts of the city, they tried to visit the Saints, hold meetings, and even continue teaching the Church Education classes at which the couple missionaries had been so effective. Sunday services continued, though the only way to get to church was to walk.

But the war moved into the center of the city. All order collapsed. Looters, hungry government troops, and rebel battalions ransacked stores and homes. If the people resisted, they were shot. Soldiers stormed through the streets, and the residents were at their mercy.

Determined to complete their missionary service, the zone

leaders, Elders Marcus Menti and Joseph Myers, devised a plan to have Brother Philip Abubkar drive to Sierra Leone with them and any of the six other local missionaries who wanted to go. Once in Sierra Leone, they could serve the last year of their mission. They faced two obstacles: they had to find the other missionaries in the area, and then they had to get out of the city.

Locating the other missionaries was not going to be easy. They were on foot, and many of the streets were strewn with dead bodies and abandoned loot. Snipers lurked in shadows, and bands of trigger-happy soldiers seemed to be everywhere.

Staying in the middle of the streets to show that they were peaceful civilians, not snipers, looters, or soldiers, they walked six miles of the main highway to the former residence of the couple missionaries. There they found four of the missing elders, who had taken refuge in the abandoned apartment. Elders Selli and Forkpah and Elders Chanipo and Gonquoi had been keeping a low profile in their own area while still visiting the members. But when the rebels ordered everyone out of the area, the missionaries had fled to the couples' apartment in what was then a safer area. The couple missionaries had left their cupboards stocked with food, which the missionaries had shared with the members.

Reunited, the six returned to the mission home, walking again in the center of the road, avoiding side streets, and keeping a steady pace so as not to call attention to themselves.

Two elders were still missing. Three local sisters volunteered to use the rebel's cease-fire break each afternoon, which allowed people to search for food, to look for the missing missionaries. Each afternoon they scouted around the pockets of heavy fighting, checking the elders' apartment and other possible hiding places. No missionaries.

At the mission home, the six missionaries, the driver, and the car, were ready to go. But the missionaries didn't know what to do about their companions.

The missing elders had been caught in the middle of the war several weeks before. They had been out doing their shopping and laundry on preparation day when gunfire erupted all around them. They rushed to their house and threw themselves to the floor. For seven hours the shooting continued. Electric power and all means of communication had been shut off by the rebels.

For a week they had stayed out of sight, bullets flying everywhere. One night during evening prayer, they heard and felt a massive explosion, followed by their neighbors calling, "Missionaries, missionaries, everyone is leaving, hurry!" They joined the throng in the street. They hadn't gone far when the rebels had stopped them to identify members of enemy tribes.

Elder Nyanforth was in no serious danger; his tribe was not at odds with the interrogators. But Elder Gaye was from a tribe considered by these rebels to be the enemy. The leaders forced everyone to squat until daylight, when identification would be easier. All night long the two elders prayed for help. Daylight came. "Though I was in an inextricable plight, I was confident of the Lord's help," Elder Gaye recalled. "What frightened us was when a man was shot by the rebels because he was Krahn. I really became fidgety and nearly collapsed." Elder Gaye was a Krahn.

Just one more person remained ahead of him in the interrogation line. For Elder Gaye, those minutes are unforgettable. "I nodded my head and began to imagine paradise. Suddenly I felt a palm on my shoulder. I dreadfully raised my head and saw that he was a Saint the Lord had sent to rescue me. He was a member of the Church who was fighting with the rebels. He knew that I was one of those being sought, but he concealed my identity from his colleagues. He forthwith told the commander that my companion and I should be released."

The rebels took the two to their refugee camp about thirteen miles from Monrovia. For a week they lived in deplorable conditions. "We fasted and prayed frequently, and we were both prompted by the Spirit to leave for Monrovia. After fervent prayer we decided to leave early Sunday morning, taking the bush road because we would now be escapees. Even though we did not know the way to town, we trusted in the Lord's help and arrived there after walking for eight hours."

In town they heard from some members that the other elders

were leaving, perhaps had already left, for Sierra Leone. Weary but hopeful, the two headed for the mission home. "We arrived after a two-hour walk just as they were putting their last bags into the boot of the car, having decided they could wait no longer for us."

The challenge now, according to Elder Gaye, was "to get nine grown men and their scant luggage into the small Toyota.

"After many stoppings, harrassings, and violent threats at gunpoint," the group arrived at the border. They had one passport—from Nigeria—to get all nine of them out of Liberia. They had no papers for the car, and their plight drew unwanted attention. They were ordered out of the car by officials who intended to confiscate the vehicle and force the group to return to Monrovia. But they remained calm.

The officials hurled insults at the missionaries and accused them of causing many of the country's political problems. Finally, one senior officer unexpectedly said, "This car belongs to a church, and these missionaries are gentlemen. Let them go."

Not out of trouble yet, the missionaries next had to barter for gas with only a small amount of cash. Again, recognizing them as missionaries, a man selling gasoline for thirty dollars a gallon dropped his price and sold them five gallons. Not enough, but it would have to do.

At times the roads deteriorated to muddy paths, but the elders forged on, sometimes running alongside the car to lighten the load and make it possible to keep going. At Kenema, Sierra Leone, they got enough fuel for the last stretch of their flight to freedom.

Just before midnight they rang the bell at the mission home. Standing on the steps before the president and his wife, Stella Rose, was a ragged band of elders who had come to labor for Zion. With food, a bath, and a good night's sleep, they were ready to go to work in their new area.

> *And they were all young men, and they were exceedingly*
> *valiant for courage, and also for strength and activity;*
> *but behold, this was not all—they were men*
> *who were true at all times.*
> Alma 53:20

# SPEAKING BAHASA

During the 1980s, the Indonesian government became concerned about the steady decline in the numbers of Muslims. Because Christian conversions were significant in that decline, all Christian churches with active proselyting programs were expelled from the country.

Missionary service by non-Indonesians and all construction for The Church of Jesus Christ of Latter-day Saints was stopped. The Church had been quietly building strength in Indonesia since 1969 when the country had been dedicated for the proclaiming of the gospel. By 1981, there were four thousand members.

Then the doors were closed, and the Indonesian Saints were left to continue with half-finished buildings and developing leadership. Ten years later, in 1991, the government reversed its edict and approved licenses of nine Christian churches whose commitment was to humanitarian welfare services. W. Dean Belnap, a retired physician, and his wife were called to reopen ties with Indonesia.

Dr. Belnap was set apart as a counselor in the Singapore mission presidency and assigned to reside in Indonesia. With no MTC language training available, he and his wife studied Bahasa, the national language, for nine months at home in Utah before leaving for Indonesia. Dr. Belnap bore his testimony at his farewell and again at his homecoming in Bahasa.

Once the Belnaps were settled in Jakarta, Dr. Belnap lectured at the college, worked with government officials, served on national committees, and conducted Church business—all in Bahasa.

He and Sister Belnap were successful in reestablishing the Church's place. "We were catching up for the years we had not been there," Dr. Belnap recalled. So well regarded were the Belnaps that he still maintains assignments with the medical school and a continuing relationship with the Indonesian Department of Education.

The Belnaps visited each unit of the Church in the country, covering more than thirty-five hundred miles every two months. They established branch and district welfare committees to solve the problems of financing education—elementary students must pay $1.50 per month and secondary students $2.50. They emphasized the law of the fast. Within a year the now five thousand members of the Church were independent in their welfare service needs.

The Belnaps also established English-language and computer classes to assist Church members. They helped open the door for family history research, which resulted in the Church gaining access to the royal lines, many of which go back to Mohammed and even further to Adam and Eve. They were influential in having the temple endowment ceremony translated into Bahasa, and they arranged to take the members of district presidencies and their wives through the Taipei Taiwan Temple.

Meanwhile, Dr. Belnap served as a visiting professor at the University of Indonesia School of Medicine. He and Sister Belnap had been admitted to the country because he was the physician in charge of a Christian medical group. But the government rescinded their permission, not wanting a "foreign physician" to be in charge of the group, and the Belnaps faced expulsion. Dr. Belnap took the problem to the Lord and was inspired to pursue affiliation with the medical school. He was welcomed to the faculty, which made it possible for him to do the work that had brought him to Indonesia—the work of the Lord. Area President John Carmack wrote, "I have never seen a missionary couple have greater impact, both with Church and with national leaders."

The Belnaps' spiritual experiences were plentiful. "We loved the people and the opportunities," said Dr. Belnap. "We were awed, as anyone would be, in observing the hand of the Lord in building his kingdom in the nation of Indonesia."

Most of all, the Belnaps loved the people. They were

"genuine, loving, simple in their needs, and appreciative of all kindness and attention." Sister Aminah Sustrisno was an example to them of the strength of the Indonesian Saints. Her story was not of conversion but of courage and determination.

She sat in her small front room. Her husband's body lay in front of her on three blocks of ice to keep it cold while the friends and family held a simple funeral service. Brother Sustrisno had died of hepatitis B, leaving his wife to raise his son, Budi, and their daughter, Yanti. The small group of mourners sitting around on the floor and on food crates sang Church hymns in tribute to the friend who had died.

Aminah's faith assured her that she would see her husband again. But the days, months and years ahead looked bleak financially. She had sold all her plates, utensils, and furniture to pay his medical bills. Fiercely independent, Aminah wanted a way to make it on her own.

Dr. Belnap had grown close to the family, and he asked Aminah how she was going to survive. She didn't know. She could cook and sell in the markets, but how could a widow with no resources and no credit get the funds to start her own business?

Dr. Belnap and local priesthood leaders recognized the need and wrestled with a way to help Aminah and others like her. Yayasan Liahona, a private foundation, was established to fund start-up cottage industries of Church members in Indonesia. Its resources were the contributions of members, not so different from the Perpetual Emigrating Fund that financed the journey across the plains of tens of thousands of Saints more than a hundred years before. What began as a small effort with Aminah as the first recipient has grown into a far-reaching organization that has helped hundreds of others. A similar system is in operation in India.

Aminah was lent $125 (U.S.), and with it she began cooking and selling sauté, rolls, and rice from a street cart in the market. The money bought the cart and her food supplies. She and her children did the rest. Her business flourished, and she repaid her advance with 2 percent interest. The funds were recycled to other Church members, who had begun timber operations and brick-making businesses as well as small home industries similar to Aminah's.

Aminah's stepson, Budi, was supported on his mission in Indonesia by Aminah's efforts. After his return, like many other LDS youth in the country, he was given access to educational grants, computer classes, and job opportunities on the rice farm purchased by the Yayasan Liahona or on its cattle operation. Once the young people have gained experience and training, they can get a job and move into the workforce. Then they can make their own way and share the gospel. Indeed, the gospel has changed their lives.

Aminah has come a long way since that day when she and other Church members gathered to pay tribute to her husband. She says, "I am making my own way and I am living the gospel. What else is there!"

> *Them hath he filled with wisdom of heart,*
> *to work all manner of work.*
> Exodus 35:35

# CALLED TO SERVE

At the laying of the cornerstone for the São Paulo Temple in March 1977, President Spencer W. Kimball invited Helvécio Martins to the podium. Brother Martins was a prominent Brazilian member of the Church, though he held no priesthood position. President Kimball counseled his friend: "What is necessary for you is faithfulness. Remain faithful, and you will enjoy all the blessings of the Church."

What could that mean for him and his family? What did it mean for Brazil? Brother Martins asked himself.

For many years, missionaries had been preaching to

Brazilians. The first elders entered the country in 1927, and over the next twenty years, 976 people joined the Church. During the 1930s and 1940s, Elder Spencer W. Kimball visited Brazil often as an ecclesiastical administrator and as a mission and stake conference visitor. And now, in the late 1970s, he was presiding at the greatest event yet: the start of the building of a temple.

Unlike many who had joined the Church in Brazil, Brother Martins and his family were neither poor nor uneducated. He had joined the Church in Rio de Janeiro. He had taken advanced studies in economics, worked in upper management for Petrobras, the largest corporation in Brazil, and taught economics at one of Brazil's most important universities. Most of his associates and friends were baffled by his dedication to the Latter-day Saint faith. They saw his church as discriminating against blacks.

Brother Martins saw it as God's church. He gave interviews to the press and worked to familiarize his countrymen with Latter-day Saint beliefs. He worked diligently in the Lord's service, even though he was not allowed to hold the priesthood. He and his wife, Ruda, the stake Primary president, spent long hours contributing to the construction of the temple, although they never expected to enter the building.

And then came the revelation, Official Declaration 2 in the Doctrine and Covenants, "extending priesthood and temple blessings to all worthy male members of the Church."

In Brazil, where forty percent of the population is black or part black, the revelation held great significance. In the Martins family, the revelation changed everything.

Brother Martins's son Marcus was nineteen years old when President Kimball announced the change on 9 June 1978. Holding the priesthood had been a dream he had never expected to realize in this life. He had not anticipated serving a mission or being married in the temple. He had joined the Church with his family on 2 July 1972 because he had believed.

Now he was engaged to a young woman who had served a mission for the Church. The invitations had been mailed for an August wedding. He was working and pursuing an engineering degree in school in Rio de Janeiro. But with the new revelation his life was transformed. On 18 June he was ordained a priest. On 25 June, an elder. And then the stake president challenged him to accept a mission call. Marcus explained his marriage plans, but the stake president didn't give in. Then the regional representative urged him to serve a mission. Marcus wrestled with the decision. His testimony was firm but so were his plans.

After much soul-searching, Marcus said yes. He was told his call would come by 22 September. But he, like the early missionaries to England who began the great pioneer migration west, felt the fire. Rather than wait for his call, he entered the missionary training center in Brazil on 5 August. The mission officials contacted Church headquarters by telephone, and he was assigned to São Paulo three days later. Marcus Martins was the first black male full-time missionary in the Church. His formal call did not come through until weeks later.

In later years, the Lord called the Martins family to significant service in his kingdom. Helvécio Martins was the first black Latter-day Saint called as a mission president, serving from 1987 to 1990 in the Brazil Fortaleza Mission. He was called as a member of the Second Quorum of Seventy in 1990. Speaking in general conference, Elder Martins spoke of his journey: "Through [our] obedience to the laws of the gospel, fasting, and service, our Heavenly Father blessed us with the power to overcome fear, challenges, and eventual adversities." (*Ensign,* Nov. 1990, 26.)

Marcus filled his mission and returned to marry his sweetheart. He enrolled at Brigham Young University in Provo, Utah, to further his academic studies and then to teach.

Today Brazil is a stronghold for the Church in South America. The pioneer spirit of the people is real, and it reaches those who are seeking the truth, as were Elder Martins and his family: "The Church of Jesus Christ of Latter-day Saints [is] the Lord's kingdom on earth, the road back to the celestial mansion of our Eternal Father." (*Ensign,* Nov. 1990, 27.)

*For we walk by faith, not by sight.*
2 Corinthians 5:7

# SWIM FOR THE BOAT

Not all the Saints who set out to cross the plains of North America reached their Zion in Utah. Those who did reach the Valley paid tribute to their dead by honoring the cause that united them, loving the Lord, and willingly serving him—come what may.

Louis Palmer had lived on the tiny island of Taaroa, French Polynesia, for only a year when he and his cousin, Tahiarii Tamarono, went out for an afternoon of fishing. It was about 4:30 when the two set off in the diesel-powered boat. The fishing was good, and in less than two hours they had a good catch. They turned toward home.

Often in the waters of the Pacific storms brew quickly. So it was that day. Waves crashed against the little boat with such force that the two fishermen were thrown into the water. The boat sputtered on without them. Brother Palmer described what happened next: "The engine was running, so we started swimming after it, hoping it would run out of diesel. After about an hour of swimming my cousin wasn't doing well. I swam back to him and said, 'We can't swim to the island. We're too far away, and it is getting dark. If you want me to stay here with you, I will.'"

His cousin replied, "No. You swim for the boat and then come back for me."

Both recognized it was their only choice. So Louis set off in the direction of the boat, deliberately pacing his strokes to conserve his strength. He said, "I don't know how long I swam. It was pitch dark, but I could hear the engine running."

He prayed as he stroked and rested. He felt he had been swimming in the ocean forever. The noise of the boat seemed to indicate it was circling, but eventually the engine ran out of diesel and stopped. Louis heard the last sputters and swam in that direction, finally reaching the silent craft. He pulled himself aboard, recognizing that he was alive through the hand of God. He took stock of the situation.

When a diesel engine runs out of fuel, recharging the fuel lines requires certain supplies. He had none. There he sat in the boat, in the dark, with a spare tank of diesel and no means to hook it up. "I just asked the Lord to bless the engine that it would start," he explained. "The first time I tried, it wouldn't start. I prayed again, and the second time, it started."

Louis went searching for his cousin. For hours he retraced his way to where he thought they had parted. He searched with no success. Getting closer and closer to the island, he finally went ashore to find help. "Many people were on the dock waiting. They were worried about us. The police came back and started searching about 2 A.M., and then at 5 A.M. another search started. They never found him."

The tragedy drew the islanders to each other and to their Father in Heaven. The next day, Sunday, the Saints gathered for a reorganization of their branch. Louis Palmer was called as the new president.

> . . . but I must cry unto my God: Thy ways are just.
> 2 Nephi 26:7

# THEN CAME THE VELVET REVOLUTION

Otakar Vojkůvka smiled at Olga Kovářová, the serious young college student so full of serious questions, and said, "God sent us to the earth to sow joy, life and love into souls." For Olga, these words were a revelation. She had grown up in Communist-controlled Czechoslovakia, but the state dogma had never seemed sound. Communist domination of society robbed people of their individuality and, hence, personality. In her world, very few seemed happy to be alive, not even herself.

Trying to find meaning in daily living and human existence,

she had taken up yoga. That had led her to this wise eighty-year-old man. "When I first visited him, I could not imagine how he had come to such a clear understanding of the true purpose of life. He talked so much of joy and peace, something in all my studies I had never heard about."

Brother Vojkůvka had been a member of the Church since before World War II. He had joined when Czechoslovakia had honored and allowed religion. He had remained faithful when the government abolished religion and directed all devotion be to the state and its newfound belief, Communism. Despite government sanctions, he had taught his family the gospel, and they, too, had remained strong and quietly devoted to God. And now he was teaching Olga, a young college student who had approached him to learn yoga. She learned much more.

"The spirit in the Vojkůvka family was something very different for me," Olga explained. She recognized that this spiritual leader had a very distinct philosophy of life that was contrary to what was practiced in their country. The two talked of beliefs that were new and captivating. On her own she'd looked for them in the New Testament, but they weren't there. "I know," Brother Vojkůvka told her and handed her a different book, a Czech translation of *A Skeptic Discovers Mormonism.*

Olga read it that night and returned with more questions. Aware of the government penalties for openly expressing interest in religion, particularly one as unknown as the Latter-day Saint religion, Olga nevertheless asked how she could contact these people and get their Book of Mormon. Brother Vojkůvka gave her the much-used family copy. Someday she would understand that many others, particularly in the early days of the Church, had come to the gospel through the words of a borrowed Book of Mormon.

She read, and each page prompted new questions. Brother Vojkůvka began to teach her, and the Spirit testified of the truth of his words. She wrote, "My first clearly spiritual experience concerned my search for a higher purpose than materialism. While reading the Book of Mormon, I came to 2 Nephi 2:25 and read,

'Adam fell that men might be; and men are, that they might have joy.' I felt as if I had discovered a lost but important understanding for which I had been searching over many years. Yes, women and men are that we might have joy! That night I suddenly awoke, sat up, and saw around me a light, and I felt the same light in my heart. I realized that no longer did I just believe in God; I knew that Heavenly Father and Jesus Christ exist. I felt their love, not only for me, not only for good people, but for all people."

Olga was converted, but with no baptismal font anywhere in Czechoslovakia, she had to wait until summer—a full six months—to be baptized. In summer they "could be in the woods and not be noticed. The police would not be expecting a religious activity in the dark," Olga said. But the baptismal party didn't count on a swarm of fisherman enjoying some evening angling. After about forty-five minutes, most of the fishermen began to pack up and go home, but too many remained on the banks of the river for Olga and her party to be safe from inquisitive eyes. Finally a brother suggested they pray and ask the Lord to intervene so Olga could be baptized. In minutes all but three of the fishermen had left, and those remaining were far enough away to pose no threat.

Later, mentioning the fisherman that evening, one brother reminded Olga of Jesus' call to Simon Peter and Andrew: "Follow me, and I will make you fishers of men." (Matthew 4:19.)

Olga was the first young convert to the Church in Czechoslovakia in forty years. At that time there were only seven other members of the Church—all of them much older than Olga. Attending her first Church gathering, Olga remembered, "I asked myself, How special is this Church? Is it only for old people?" As she soon learned, most young Church members had escaped from Czechoslovakia before Communist control could lock them in. Brother Vojkůvka told her of being questioned many times over the years and of government reports about him that warned: "Be careful. This man has a great influence on young people." Olga recognized that she "would soon be an instrument in God's hands to bring young people into the Church."

Membership in the Church put all of them at great risk. Olga described their tense situation: "We dared to meet only in the evening, at first once a month, and later once a week, when it was already dark outside and the neighbors were occupied with doing something other than being interested in people gathering. The blinds were pulled down, the windows had to stay closed, and we did not sing hymns for fear of being overheard. In these meetings, however, we strongly felt the Holy Ghost."

Despite the danger, the group of believers grew, and by 1989 they numbered more than sixty; Olga's parents were converted soon after she was. Recalling those days Olga said, "We had only one Book of Mormon among us; it was more than forty years old, from before the time of Communism. The neighbors, noticing the many visits, wondered why their elderly neighbor, Mr. Vojkůvka, had so many young friends. Once a neighbor asked him, 'Mr. Vojkůvka, what do you celebrate each Sunday? So many young people are coming to your house.' He answered simply, 'We learn to be happy.' After the revolution in 1989 the neighbor returned to say, 'I think that I too need your school of life.'"

During the era of Communist control, Olga became a teacher with a doctoral degree in education and pedagogy. She served as the leader of the Ethics and Morality Department of the Children and Young People Center at Masaryk University in Brno, Czechoslovakia. Professionally as well as personally she was focused on a better life, convinced that "we must learn to think of life as something beyond simply having enough good food to eat. We must become a moral people."

For forty years her country had become used to a godless, pleasure-seeking mentality. Wanting to change that perspective, Olga introduced within the university system her different way of life. She devised a seven-point plan that she taught in her classes, incorporated as the thesis of a textbook, and explained in a newsletter distributed on campus. These same seven points were part of a teaching plan at yoga camps that Olga and the Vojkůvka family ran in the summers.

"The points are really quite simple," said Olga. When she

showed them to a colleague at the university, he laughed at them. But when he attended one of her classes, he was amazed at the enthusiasm of the young people. Olga identified the points to "help youth build meaningful relationships with others and to bring them to see a better side of life, a more spiritual life." Suddenly these students who had been starved for spiritual things all their lives had something to believe in. Said Olga, "We taught university students seven ideas: first, admiration for good things in life; second, self-respect; third, being interested in living; fourth, finding joy in living; fifth, expressing gratitude; sixth, loving others (as Jesus intended); and seventh, enthusiasm—finding the burning within."

The Czech youth, forced to follow Communist practices and give lip service to its tenets, were cynical. They had become discouraged and apathetic, living with no thought beyond the moment. Olga offered something new.

She was questioned by the secret police many times, but they were kind to her. Sometimes she could tell by their carefully phrased questions that they knew she was a Church member, but since the Church members did not organize or teach against the government she felt relatively safe.

And she was successful.

When the Communist grip was broken, the people were ready to receive the missionaries. Olga's father was called as branch president of the Uherske Hradiste Branch where, in 1991, after only two years of missionary work, there were eighty-two members.

Wrote Olga of that singular time, "After forty years of an alien history, a history imposed on us by another nation, the history of the Czech people resumed."

*Where the Spirit of the Lord is, there is liberty.*
2 Corinthians 3:17

# "WHEN YE ARE LEARNED"

At first, Fan Hsieh listened to the Latter-day Saint missionaries because he was curious. And he was polite. He invited them back after finding that he enjoyed their conversations. One day he asked the elders why their church didn't have crosses or crucifixes. They replied, "Because Christ is risen; Christ lives. If one of your friends or parents dies, do you take out a photograph of them dead and show it to everyone?" This wisdom caught Hsieh off guard, and he determined to learn more.

Diligently advancing in knowledge was the essence of his life. As a child in the rural farming community of Tayeh, China, Hsieh did not attend school until he was ten. At age fourteen, he enrolled in a Catholic school where, in addition to academic subjects, he was taught of Jesus Christ and was soon baptized a Catholic. "I saw the example of many good Catholic missionaries," he later said, "and I thought maybe China needed more of them to teach the people about Jesus Christ."

Hsieh decided to become a priest. His advanced studies took him to the Catholic seminary in Wuhan for four years and then to the Catholic University in Beijing. When the Communists overran the city in 1949, he fled to Shanghai and became a student at Aurora Jesuit University. The Communist march continued, and Hsieh transferred to the Catholic seminary in Hong Kong, which relocated to Macao. There Hsieh was ordained a priest.

His service was called for in Rome, where he studied Italian, Latin, and law for four years. He moved to Paris and continued his study of languages: French, Greek, Hebrew, English, Spanish, and German. His goal was to learn more of Jesus Christ through reading original sources and texts.

The next logical step came in 1967, when he was appointed a member of the faculty at the Fu Jen Catholic University of Taipei as a teacher of philosophy and French. This was a setting where he could share his belief and testimony of Jesus Christ.

But Hsieh was uneasy about his direction. Though he valued the process of learning, some of his knowledge caused him concern. "I spent eighteen years teaching and fulfilling my responsibilities as a priest," he said. "I was very busy, but I wasn't happy. I had the opportunity to study in Europe; I had been a teacher, a student, a professor, a chaplain, a seminary director—my life was colorful—but there was a spiritual void."

To him, some Catholic customs seemed flawed. The pursuit of knowledge, for instance, was hampered by a ban on certain books. Hsieh's need for companionship seemed reinforced by the scripture in Genesis 2:18: "It is not good that the man should be alone." Indeed, Hsieh believed that caution. "This scripture became a vivid reality for me. Once when I was seriously sick and there was no one close to take care of me, I felt very alone. I realized the need for a companion to share my life. I decided then that being alone forever wasn't right."

Hsieh recognized that he either had to continue to ignore his feelings or find another path for his life. He chose the latter. In 1973 he left the Catholic priesthood and resigned his post at Fu Jen University. He was immediately put on the faculty at the national Cheng Chi University in Taipei. He started looking for a wife and married one of his university assistants.

Three years later the Latter-day Saint missionaries knocked on his door. He had no time for them, but something prompted him to go to his balcony and wave them back. They set up an appointment, which prompted Hsieh's wife to caution her husband, "beware of false prophets." (Matthew 7:15.)

But the door was open and Hsieh was prepared for the true gospel. He met often with the elders and was interested in the simplicity of their beliefs and their answers to his questions. They lent him books by Church authorities, which he studied carefully. When they spoke of their priesthood, he saw an opportunity to be part of the true priesthood of God.

Hsieh and his wife investigated the Church together, and they were baptized together in December 1977. "We've always tried to use every opportunity and every talent he has given us to help build up the kingdom of God on the earth and to share the gospel message."

Brother Hsieh's contributions are legion. He lectured seven times at the International Conference for Christian professors, bearing his testimony to scholars. He served in the Taipei Taiwan Temple presidency and on the high council of the Taipei Taiwan West Stake. His language skills have been put to good use in helping with a second Chinese translation of the Book of Mormon.

For one who had spent his life in search of knowledge and truth, Brother Hsieh had finally found it: "What we do, we do for the glory of God and the salvation of souls. Friendship is the method by which we share the gospel. The final goal for all is salvation and exaltation."

*Put on the new man, which is renewed in knowledge*
*after the image of him that created him.*
Colossians 3:10

# JAILED FOR PROSELYTING

Four sister missionaries and the president of the Greece Athens Mission were traveling north to cross the border into Macedonia (Yugoslavia). It was 2 June 1993, and the missionaries needed new visas. The missionaries had been denied an extension of their residence permits, and this was the only feasible way to remain in Greece. So they planned to travel out of the country and back in again, picking up their new visas the next day as they reentered Greece.

This time, the party leaving the country was to be joined by the four missionaries serving in Thessaloniki. They, too, needed new permits. The plans were well detailed, but the mission president didn't count on the four elders in Thessaloniki being arrested and thrown in jail for "street boarding." Since its beginnings, the Church has faced persecution, its members and its missionaries sometimes being threatened with violence and imprisonment.

This was not the first time missionaries had been charged by the police with proselyting, a criminal offense, since the Greece Athens Mission was opened on 1 July 1990. Usually the arrests were the results of misunderstandings that took long hours to work out, but they had always been resolved at the station.

President R. Douglas Phillips recalled an incident when two elders were out knocking on doors. A deacon of the Greek Orthodox Church approached them and said, "Go to Africa. Go to America. Don't teach here, for we have a religion. Leave our country." In a few minutes, police officers arrived and the elders were arrested and charged with proselyting.

Several hours later, after the authorities had shuttled between the clerics of the Greek Orthodox Church and the missionaries, they determined that the proselyting law had not been violated. But the missionaries were not free to leave. The police wanted to see that all the foreign missionaries' papers were in order, and the process dragged late into the night. Eventually they were released and reminded not to proselyte.

But the incident with the four elders in Thessaloniki was the first in three years to go to court.

President Phillips and the district leader found the four missionaries at the police station. The police had charged them with proselyting, claiming that numerous individuals had complained. The missionaries explained that they had been arrested after being approached by persons who turned out to be plainclothes police. The head of the department was one of them, and he was firm about keeping the missionaries in jail.

When the mission president asked to use the phone to call an attorney, he was told the police phone did not allow long-distance calls and he was sent outside to a kiosk to phone the Athens attorney the mission had used. The United States consul for Thessaloniki, Frank Collins, went to the station to meet with the police, but the mission president was excluded from the conversations.

Then it was announced that a hearing would be held that evening at 6 P.M. at the main courthouse. The missionaries were to present their passports at that time. The afternoon was filled with taking taxis around the city to gather the passports from the missionaries' apartments.

Present at the pretrial hearing was the mission president, the district leader, and Mr. Katsios, an associate of the Athens counsel, Mr. Mavros. President Phillips described what happened:

"The four missionaries were brought by four plainclothes police from the hall where they had been photographed and fingerprinted. After some time, Mr. Katsios went into the office of a judge. . . . After about fifteen minutes, I was invited in and asked if we should have an immediate trial the next day or postpone the trial for two months. Since Mr. Mavros, our attorney, had already made arrangements to fly to Thessaloniki that evening, I felt it advisable to proceed immediately with the trial. Furthermore, since I was scheduled to be released from my assignment within a month, I did not wish to leave the case unresolved for the new mission president."

Arriving at the courthouse the next morning were Mr. Katsios's assistant, Elder and Sister Thorn, a missionary couple, the four sister missionaries, Rosa, a Church member who had brought food to the imprisoned elders, and a new convert, Despoina Hatzopoulou. Her presence was fortuitous because she, being a physician and therefore a professional, was allowed to translate at the trial.

The trial began at 2:30 P.M. with the police testifying first. Then President Phillips was called to the stand and, after being asked to swear on the Bible, was informed he could make his statement.

"I explained that first of all I was not a professional cleric but a professor of Greek and Latin at an American university and was assigned for three years as a mission president. I also informed the court that the missionaries were not professional ministers but that most were college students who are called for two years. I emphasized that they come to Greece voluntarily, that they love the Greek people, and that when they return to the United States they become unofficial ambassadors for Greece.

"I then testified that we were desirous of obeying the law and that, according to the information we had, we were not in violation. I recounted that we were informed by a security policeman from the Ambelokipi police station in Athens, who had visited me more than two years before, that proselytizing was to deceive, manipulate, pressure, or bribe someone in an attempt to persuade them to change their religion and that missionaries do not employ these practices or tactics."

President Phillips gave some background on the Church represented by the missionaries, explaining that its millions of members lived in almost every country in the world, except Muslim countries. He also explained that fifty thousand missionaries, like the four on trial, serve for two years at their own expense. One of the prosecutors asked, "How would you feel if Greek Orthodox missionaries went to your homeland?" The president answered, "They would be free to come and would be welcomed."

When it was the missionaries' turn to testify, they explained what they were doing when they were arrested.

The judge deliberated very briefly with his associates and then announced his verdict: Not guilty.

> *We are troubled on every side, yet not distressed; we are*
> *perplexed, but not in despair; persecuted, but not*
> *forsaken; cast down, but not destroyed.*
> 2 Corinthians 4:8–9

---

# REMEMBERING HOT DOGS AND SAUERKRAUT

War teaches many lessons: some on the battlefront, some in the heart. Twenty-year-old private A. C. Christensen saw six months of combat in World War II before being captured and sent to a Japanese prison camp. Early in his captivity he was forced to relinquish almost all of his few possessions. When a guard eyed his watch, about the only thing he had left, he understood the signal. He removed the watch from his wrist and handed it over.

He spent the next three years in a daily routine of endless beatings, exhaustion, disease, and death. Hunger was his constant companion; he struggled to remember even the most simple meals of hot dogs and sauerkraut on board ship.

Like those pioneers who pushed and pulled when their feet were bare and their strength gone, their companions lost to death and disease, somehow he carried on.

But eventually that strength began to wane, and finally he found himself slipping toward death as so many of his fellow soldiers had done. "They weren't necessarily the sickest among us," he recalled, "but they would lie in their beds in a semifetal position and stare at nothing." At morning bed check they were dead.

"Death began to seem more and more like my only release. One day I put down my hammer and told the guard I would not work any longer. I didn't care what he did to me. I wanted to die. He beat me, and afterwards, as I lay in my bed waiting for the end to come, I took out the two precious pieces of paper I had managed to keep concealed for three years: one was a picture of my parents, the other was my patriarchal blessing.

"As I read my blessing, I thought of my grandfather, the patriarch who had given me the blessing, and my dear mother, who had patiently taken down every word. The words softened me. Maybe there was a future for me after all. Then I studied my parents' faces in the picture. I began to recall my childhood, our farm, my brother Max, and the times we had spent riding our horses.

"I started to pray. Somehow I began to feel strengthened. I remembered that Helaman's army of two thousand had been strengthened by their mothers' teachings. I remembered my mother's words to me and my brother, both still in our late teens. She promised us that if we would always live the Word of Wisdom, the Lord would bless us.

"As I lay there thinking about what my mother had said, I weighed only eighty-five pounds. I didn't feel that I could run and not be weary, but maybe I could walk and not faint. That day my spirits lifted, and I determined that I would hang on.

"I had beaten my enemy."

> *Be patient in afflictions, for thou shalt have many;*
> *but endure them, for, lo, I am with thee.*
> Doctrine and Covenants 24:8

# WHATEVER IS NEEDED

Establishing an official Church presence in Czechoslovakia had been impossible. The government officials responsible for such decisions were cold, not interested, and not attentive. For many years the request for official recognition was studied. And later, "still being studied." Then in February 1990, the key unyielding official was removed, and his successor "had ears to hear."

Elder Russell M. Nelson had for many years tried to open a dialogue with government officials in Czechoslovakia. He told of finally arriving at a time when a receptive official "heard our complete story. He said, 'Your request for recognition will be approved this very month. Your people may again worship in full dignity. Your missionaries may again return to this country.'" Official recognition was granted 21 February and became effective 1 March 1990.

The courageous efforts of the district president in Czechoslovakia, Jiři Šnederfler, whom Elder Nelson called "the real hero of the story," were vital in the Church's obtaining official recognition. He explained:

"Some two and one-half years earlier, Elder Ringger and I had learned that recognition could be formally requested only by a Czechoslovakian member of the Church. So we went to the home of Brother and Sister Šnederfler. We explained that we had just received that information from the chairman of the Council of Religious Affairs. Knowing that other Czechoslovakian leaders and thinkers had been imprisoned or put to death for religious or dissident belief, we told Brother Šnederfler that we, as his Church leaders, could not and would not make that request of him. After contemplating only a brief moment, Brother Šnederfler humbly said, 'I will go! I will do it!' As he spoke, his wife, Olga, shed a tear. They embraced and said, 'We will do whatever is needed. This is for our Lord, and His work is more important than our freedom or life.'

"Some months later, when the papers were properly prepared, Brother Šnederfler submitted them personally. He and other members were subjected to strict surveillance. The Saints continued in courage and faith. Ultimately, after periodic fasting and prayer and complete compliance with all requirements, they received that glorious announcement of recognition. How I admire the Šnederflers and all those stalwart members who endured so much interrogation and risk."

Brother and Sister Šnederfler did not rest. Brother Šnederfler was called to preside over the Freiberg Germany Temple, beginning 1 September 1991, and Sister Šnederfler was called as the temple matron.

*No one can assist in this work except he shall be*
*humble and full of love, having faith, hope,*
*and charity, being temperate in all things,*
*whatsoever shall be entrusted to his care.*
Doctrine and Covenants 12:8

# YOU DON'T CHANGE YOUR RELIGION

Every year the parents of Vadakke Madu Harihara Subramoniam Iyer (Ganesh) acknowledge their eldest son at a death anniversary rite. Ganesh, reared in an orthodox Hindu family with priestly Brahman lineage, is dead to his family because he joined The Church of Jesus Christ of Latter-day Saints.

Ganesh is not alone. Young converts in India are frequently disowned and expelled from their homes. Changing religion is an extraordinary breach with culture and family practices. India Bangalore Mission president Gurcharan Singh Gill explained: "The concept that you don't change your religion is so prevalent in this society that when young people join the Church, they often lose the respect and association of their parents and their portion of the family inheritance."

The LDS Church in India and neighboring Pakistan, Bangladesh, and Sri Lanka is at about the stage where the Church was forty or fifty years ago in South America. Religious culture is so much a part of the lifestyle that it is difficult for a person to adopt another religion. That families are still a primary force in that region strengthens the Church's effort but also makes it difficult for those converted to break with the family's religious tradition. So it was for Ganesh.

In 1986 in Goa, a town overlooking India's west coast and the Arabian Sea, Ganesh and a group of his friends were working to have India declared a religious state. Ganesh was assigned to collect material about the LDS Church and to dissuade LDS missionaries from actively promoting their religion. That's how he met Laurel and Nathel Hill from Ogden, Utah. The Hills were holding discussions in their home to introduce the Church and its principles to those who were interested. At that time open proselyting in India was against the law.

Meeting with the missionaries did not go as Ganesh expected. "I loved Christians," he explained, "but I hated them for the work they were doing. We felt that they were polluting India, and we wanted to stop conversions to Christianity."

In his first few meetings, Ganesh talked with the Hills about a wide range of subjects. He found himself intrigued with their knowledge, their openness, their sincerity. "Each time we spoke I forgot what I went to talk to them about," he recalled. After three visits he abandoned his opposition and began earnestly to learn from them. In one of those visits the Hills gave Ganesh a copy of the Book of Mormon and then taught him to pray. Soon after, while on a three-month assignment for his work, Ganesh became quite ill. He decided to pray for help in regaining his health, and he turned to the Lord. He got better.

When he returned to Goa, he began taking the missionary discussions. So intrigued was he that his after-work discussions stretched late into the night as he probed the truths of the gospel. After the fifth discussion, Brother Hill challenged Ganesh to be baptized, and he accepted. "We both wept," Ganesh said.

The news of his conversion was not well received. His friends who had set out with him to rid the country of other religions were stunned. "I told them I was not happy with the work I was doing earlier, but that I was happy now," says Ganesh. "And then I got the same treatment that I had caused others to get, which means I got beaten up on the road, twice, very nicely."

That was just the beginning. Ganesh was fired from his job and forced to move from his apartment. His parents' disowned him and stripped him of all rights in the family. They said, "We don't want you to be a member of our family. You became a Christian missionary. We can never forgive you for that."

Though the family attempted to sever all ties, Ganesh tried to maintain some contact. A serious illness that hospitalized his mother opened a way for him to share his faith and religion. The family posted a guard outside her hospital room to keep Ganesh from seeing her. Ganesh, however, walked unrecognized into his mother's room and asked her if she would like a blessing.

"You bless me?" she asked, because in Hinduism, only the elders bless those younger. Ganesh explained the purpose of priesthood blessings, and his mother consented. He felt prompted to bless her with renewed health, and within days she was released from the hospital.

"She appreciated what I had done. She told me, 'I know that you are in the right place for you.' That's enough for me." When Ganesh got married, she wanted to go to the wedding. In fact, she approved of his wife, but no one else did. And no one from his family attended his wedding.

Ganesh's father believed that if God had wanted Ganesh to be a member of the LDS Church, his son would have been born into the Church. So many hopes were tied up in this eldest son. Ganesh said his father "thought I would take care of and bring up the family's name, I being the first son. As per his calculation, I am not doing that. But I told him I believe that God has a purpose for me: to put me where I was and to put me where I am now. I know, because of my patriarchal blessing, that my ancestors will be grateful for the work I will do for them.

"I will be forever grateful to my Heavenly Father because, to use my earthly father's words, 'I am what I am and not what I was.'"

*Watch ye, stand fast in the faith . . . be strong.*
1 Corinthians 16:13

# LEFT TO CARRY ON

In the late 1930s The Church of Jesus Christ of Latter-day Saints was struggling in France. Neighboring Germany had quickly built membership, but France had had a much slower start. Then World War II broke out, and the Church withdrew its missionaries. The mission records describe the time: "During the last week of August, while world peace seems lost, and in accordance with the wishes of the First Presidency, the missionaries in France are invited to go toward the cities that are ports or cities that allow contact with ports. Before leaving our meeting place in Paris on 3 September 1939, and after one of the most beautiful meetings, we read the alarming headlines in the newspaper that England had declared war on Germany in the morning and that France had followed suit in the afternoon."

Convert Leon Fargier was left to carry on.

He took the assignment seriously. Belgian Latter-day Saint Gaston Chappuis, who had been assigned to close the mission office in Paris, gave Leon the special charge: "You are the only active member of the priesthood in France. I know that you will do your best and will use the talent that the Lord has given you."

He did. Through the war years he was the LDS spiritual leader for all of France. He baptized and confirmed new members, blessed the sick, and visited and visited. He held meetings, administered the sacrament, and encouraged his fellow Saints with his indomitable faith.

He wrote in his journal of the challenges. "After France was divided in two, I traveled to give the sacrament to some sisters in Bouches-du-Rhône, to hold sacrament meetings once a month in Lyon and Valence, to visit the members in Lyon and Saint-Etienne, and to meet in their home. In Valence, our building being occupied by refugees, I held meetings in my home. During this period I was studying ways to get to the other side into the occupied zone in order to visit the members, but this was not always easy."

Nothing about being a member of the Church in France was easy. When Leon joined the Church in 1932, the missionaries were finding few to listen to their message. The missionary force in the country had been cut by two-thirds because of the slow progress. When Leon and his wife, Claire, joined the Church, the Valence branch membership jumped by 40 percent—from five to seven members!

Leon wrote: "It was in Valence that I felt myself attracted to God, and I was also led by his power toward the Mormon missionaries. Before meeting them, I had never had any knowledge of the Bible. At the time, in the morning, I was going to meetings of the Salvation Army and in the evening to the meetings of the Church of Jesus Christ. After I had prayed, God revealed to me the truth that is found in The Church of Jesus Christ of Latter-day Saints, and I was baptized by Robert Hulle on 13 August 1932 and confirmed by him. My wife was baptized the same day by Ivan Jones and confirmed by Herbert Merrill."

After his baptism in a municipal swimming pool, Leon was

immediately called as a missionary and was later ordained a teacher, a priest, and then an elder by mission president Octave F. Ursenbach on 30 May 1936.

President Heber J. Grant visited southern France, and Leon shook the prophet's hand. In 1937, inspired by the visit of the Lord's prophet, the members of the fledgling branch placed two thousand tracts and drew attention to the Book of Mormon in street exhibits.

Leon began his ministry when the Church withdrew the missionaries. "I went to Besançon and to Paris, in 1944. I continued my visits to Nîmes, Saint-Florent, Saint-Etienne, and Grenoble, but the precariousness of the trains hampered things a great deal. On 12 November 1944 I recommenced the meetings in Grenoble, Nimes and Saint-Etienne. . . . [I visited] Brother Bret in Montrigaud (to ordain him to the office of deacon), where I had to return on foot a distance of twenty-nine kilometers [about eighteen miles] to Romans."

Leon grew accustomed to walking and to riding a bike. His Church work drew attention from the Vichy government, which was closely tied to the Germans, and Leon was told to stop his religious activity.

He didn't.

Newspapers wrote of his commitment. The major national daily paper, *Paris-Soir,* wrote in a front-page article: "Mr. Fargier, the only Mormon pastor in the free zone, has baptized fifteen of his flock in the municipal swimming pool in Grenoble." He was tireless in his attention to the Lord's work and was often arrested by the Gestapo for his efforts, yet he continued.

Wrote Leon: "Valence underwent intense bombing, and we had to take refuge along with Brother and Sister Margel in the home of friends in the country, where we stayed until Valence was taken by the Americans. . . . It is useless to mention all the suffering endured throughout this war in which we have suffered hunger and the presence of the occupying forces. . . . I thank God for having preserved my family from all of these calamities."

At the close of the war, Leon was called as a missionary in

his branch and later as branch president. He bore his testimony to Elder Ezra Taft Benson, who spent a year in Europe representing the Church and overseeing its efforts to contribute to rebuilding postwar Europe.

Brother and Sister Fargier were present when President David O. McKay dedicated the Swiss Temple, and then they attended the temple themselves. "We received our endowments, and our marriage was sealed for eternity on 14 September [1955]. From that time until . . . November 1957 we went to the temple seven times to do the work for those who have left us."

*Be diligent unto the end. Pray always, that you may come off conqueror; yea, that you may conquer Satan, and that you may escape the hands of the servants of Satan that do uphold his work.*
Doctrine and Covenants 10:4–5

# PATIENCE AND CHARITY

Maintaining life and adapting to the frontier consumed much of the pioneers' energies during their first years in Zion. From their own struggles they learned patience; from the trials of others they learned to share what little they had.

In general conference in 1856 word came that handcart pioneers were stranded on the trail, freezing in the early winter storms. The members responded. "The sisters stripped of their Peticoats stockings and every thing they could spare, right there in the Tabernacle, and piled [them] into the wagons to send to the Saints in the Mountains." (Lucy Meserve Smith, in Jill Mulvay Derr, Janath Russell Cannon, and Maureen Ursenbach Beecher, *Women of Covenant: The Story of Relief Society* [Salt Lake City: Deseret Book, 1992], 77.)

President Brigham Young called for men, wagons, and relief supplies. (See *Journal of Discourses,* 26 vols. [London: Latter-day Saints' Book Depot, 1854–86], 4:112–19.) Twenty-seven young men with 16 four-mule teams set out almost immediately to rescue the incoming Saints. By the end of the month, 250 teams were on the trail, carrying the clothing, quilts, blankets, flour, vegetables, and fruit that were desperately needed by the westering companies delayed by early snowfall.

With patience and charity, modern-day pioneers too are called to sacrifice, set their faces to the wind, and carry on. They make do with what they have, sharing not only their resources but their energy and commitment with each other. And in the process, they too come to Zion.

# NURSE THIS LITTLE PLOT

In August 1995, Julia Mavimbela of Soweto, South Africa, was honored by Brigham Young University at its commencement exercises. Her citation was for "outstanding contribution to a profession, a community, a religion." Sister Mavimbela was indeed qualified for such a tribute.

Julia Mavimbela had earned a teaching certificate in the late 1930s when educational opportunities for black women in South Africa were severely limited. She had supported herself and her mother on her small salary of five pounds every three months. She took seriously her charge to educate her students, and her efforts reached beyond the classroom. Unknown to her supervisors, she taught a class of forty students who were too poor to attend her school. She was a capable administrator as well as teacher and became one of the first women principals in her country. In addition, she established soup kitchens for parents and a community thrift program called Waste Not, Want Not, decades before such programs became popular.

In 1976, while grieving over the death of her husband in an accident caused by a drunken driver, Julia was dismayed by the riots that ripped at the core of her country. Schools were closed, students took to the streets, and buildings were being burned.

She developed a plan "to try to engage the hand, to engage the mind" of the youngsters who would otherwise be caught up in the violence. Working mainly with children aged four to ten, Julia created a garden on an abandoned and garbage-strewn lot. Like the early pioneers in Utah, she understood that working with the soil not only produces harvests but heals souls. She put the children to work preparing the ground for planting. "See what good things you can grow if you nurse this little plot," she said. Her ideas were planted in other hearts, and soon little gardens, some as small as closets, were popping up all over the community.

As Julia and the youngsters cleared the weeds, she taught them about the value of work, the beauty of nature, the law of the harvest—and in between she taught them to read. She started with the seed packages. From *carrots* came two words. On an abandoned car on the premises she painted the word *car,* and on the compost heap she placed a sign labeled *rot.* Her homegrown vocabulary lessons sprouted alongside the carrots and beans in the abandoned lot.

Water for the garden was kitchen waste water, and when that supply was insufficient, she would turn to her students and say, "Come. Let's go home. Let's all pray—we'll surely see something happen." Often it did. The next morning she would come to the patch, and a good rain would have soaked the ground overnight. She said, "I can't tell you of the excitement I saw in those beautiful little faces, all convinced that surely there was someone interested in and caring for the work they were doing."

Her efforts did not go unnoticed. A South African publication paid tribute to the gardens: "Mrs. Mavimbela dreams and schemes to get the youth involved in making Soweto greener . . . to make them feel that their surroundings belong to them and that they are responsible for them—and therefore will not destroy them. She wishes to repair not only the physical damage of the recent riots, but also the mental and moral damage, and her message to youth is, 'Where there was a bloodstain, a beautiful flower must grow.'"

In 1981 her consuming drive to improve the lives of children and families brought her face to face with two American elders who had a message to share.

Because of her prominence in many causes in the community, some Anglican women had approached Julia to "clean up the Dube Boys' Club which was in terrible shape." She wasn't persuaded. Their interest in the boys and their claim to need her help didn't ring true, and she refused. But the next morning she had a change of heart and stopped by to check on the club for herself. "I noticed two white boys (as I called them), greeted them, and asked them what they were doing. They said they were helping, and I asked, Why? Where do you come from?"

"From America," they explained and then followed her about in her business of assessing the situation at the club. When they proposed visiting her in her home, she was surprised. "At that time in Soweto whoever admitted a white into his home was considered a traitor." Intending to put them off, she said, "Give me three days to go and clean my little house. I'm a woman who is always on the street, and cobwebs are hanging."

The missionaries were not dissuaded. Three days later they appeared at her door and Julia let them in. When she read *Elder* on the name tags, she shivered, for in her church "an elder was an untouchable" and she had just let two into her house. They presented the first discussion; she was not impressed, dismissing their message as "just from another one of those groups that come to preach to us." The second discussion, the next week, was the same. That she even was continuing to talk to them surprised her, but she felt something in her heart for the young men and allowed them back a third time.

That time, "they looked on the wall at the wedding photo of my husband and me. They wanted to know where he was, and I told them that he had died. This time they kindled a spark of interest in me. They asked, 'Did you know that you can have someone be baptized for him?' I want to tell you, my eyes opened wide because I had been taught that it was improper even to speak of someone who had died," Julia replied. "It is strange to hear you whites talk about the dead as if they were alive."

She asked to learn more of their doctrine. Two months later she was baptized on the anniversary of the day her father had died, a date set before she recognized its family significance. Later she not only had the baptismal work done for her husband but she was sealed to him in the Johannesburg South Africa Temple.

Joining the Church did not bring great change into her

lifestyle. But how it extended her reach and put all her efforts into a new perspective! This gracious yet forceful white-haired grandmother, fluent in seven languages, explained her now-broadened perspective: "My message is the whole world was given by Heavenly Father for us to live in peace. Color is not a criterion. We're all children of God, and if we recognize the scriptures and the plan of salvation, then we'll know what it means to love our brothers as ourselves."

Sister Mavimbela, who has served in the Soweto Branch as the Relief Society president and as a Gospel Doctrine teacher, has been on the frontier of change for years. She has served as vice-president of the National Council of Women of South Africa, the first black woman elected to that post, and she has maintained her commitment to the Women for Peace movement she helped found and direct for many years. She has sponsored literacy programs and homemaking clubs, lobbied officials for changes in laws and, as progress came, kept on lobbying. She has been a peaceful force for change in a country where many issues are fought in the streets.

Sister Mavimbela has worked side by side with both black women and white women to improve lives, of children in particular, and to revive hope. To a huge audience of women at the Brigham Young University Women's Conference in 1990 she said, "I give thanks to God that he has made me a woman. I give thanks to my creator that he has made me black; that he has fashioned me as I am, with hands, heart, head to serve my people. It can, it should, be a glorious thing to be a woman. It is important for women to be aware of their common lot. It is important for women to stand together and rise together to meet our common enemies—illiteracy, poverty, crime, disease, and stupid, unjust laws that have women feel so helpless as to be hopeless."

Others see Sister Mavimbela as a leader of hearts and minds, a teacher with great purpose and perspective, an example to everyone who is touched by her hand. She sees herself as a child of God.

*Wherefore, I love little children with a perfect love.*
Moroni 8:17

# WITH THE LORD NOTHING IS IMPOSSIBLE

The two Hungarian women, a mother and daughter, were ready for baptism. When the missionaries asked if they would commit to become members of The Church of Jesus Christ of Latter-day Saints, the mother answered, "Yes, I suppose I know I must." Without a word, her thirty-year-old daughter nodded her agreement.

Only a few months before, the Hungarian government had not allowed baptisms. The missionaries recalled the controversy with officials when they had tried to use the swimming pool at the hotel. But those restrictions had been lifted, and now they could take converts into the waters of baptism.

If they had a font.

Much of missionary work is simply having faith and taking the next step. So the two missionaries set a date a little more than two weeks off and then began to look for a place to baptize their investigators.

The Church in Hungary was just getting started. For several months, the ten members in the Budapest Branch, the only Saints among the 2.5 million residents of the Hungarian capital, had met in the missionaries' tiny apartment. But they had outgrown their small quarters, and the mission president was looking for a permanent place for Church meetings.

Although being baptized in a lake, river, pond, or even the ocean would place the new converts squarely in the tradition of Saints and pioneers the world over, that wasn't an option for these two Hungarian women. The Danube River, at its peak and with fierce currents, was far too risky for the sixty-year-old mother, and the weather had turned bitter cold. The indoor pool the missionaries had used before had been drained and covered. So the missionaries talked with their mission president and followed his advice: they prayed.

The baptism day drew closer. Still no appropriate pool had

been located, though the search for a meetinghouse had been successful. Elder Christopher J. H. Jones recalled, "The Church bought a large house in the hills of Budapest, large enough for Church meetings. Now we had the building, but we still had no font."

The elders discussed the problem with the two investigators, but the women seemed undaunted. They were committed to baptism and had faith the Lord would provide a way. Each time the missionaries uneasily brought up the question of the font, the daughter told them, "We Hungarians keep our commitments. God will keep his."

He did.

Only days before the scheduled service, the mission president telephoned the elders. "I am coming to see you. And I am bringing your font."

He arrived with a portable font loaded in the back of his car. Found in a basement in Germany, the font had been driven in relays to Budapest. "It took two days to transport it, two hours to set it up, and fifteen hours to fill it with water. But it was a font," wrote Elder Jones.

The baptism, the first function in the new meetinghouse of the Church in Budapest, was held on schedule. The water in the font was tinged with rust from the pipes. A wobbly chair draped with a sheet was used for the women to sit on while being confirmed. The guests sat on the stairs. Because the building had not been used recently, there was no electricity. Candles lighted the room, and the guests sang familiar hymns—"Praise God from Whom All Blessings Flow" and "A Mighty Fortress Is Our God." They sang without accompaniment when the batteries of the small cassette recorder failed early in the service. It didn't matter.

Elder Jones said, "It was a moment none of us will ever forget," a moment only those who "lay aside the things of this world, and seek for the things of a better" will ever know. (D&C 25:10.)

*And this because of their exceeding faith, and their*
*patience in their tribulations.*
Alma 60:26

# "A PREMEDITATED APOSTATE"

Mary Barton planned to marry in the temple and rear her family in The Church of Jesus Christ of Latter-day Saints. A former Quaker, then convert, then LDS missionary, she was firm in that resolve until she received the strong impression that she should marry Jim Kirk, a friend from Quaker boarding school. He had written to her while she was serving her mission in Montreal, "I hear you are pretty badly brainwashed, and I am going to have to come and save you from this terrible thing."

After her mission she took a job near the boarding school in Ohio. Jim's farm was not far away. Both of them loved the farm and were well suited to the long hours and hard work a success-ful farm required. So for many months Mary worked at the hard-ware store in town and helped Jim with the garden, even baling hay in her free time. She understood his passion for the farm; it reminded her of her feelings for the gospel. He said to her one night, "Sometimes I wish I could just hug the whole farm at once."

Mary worried that she was "becoming a premeditated apostate," but "we went so well together. It's like we were already one; the paperwork just hadn't been done." But she had so many questions: How could she be feeling right about doing something that would take her away from the Church she had embraced so fully? In studying Church teachings and Church history, she rec-ognized the power of a husband and wife coming into the Church together. Many of the early pioneers had left their families and their religious roots to follow the teachings of latter-day prophets. But most of the stories she had heard were of the partners being committed to the Church—together.

"Jim wasn't hot on the idea of becoming a member," Mary wrote in her journal. In fact, he told her bluntly he had no inter-est in the Church. Yet when she prayed for guidance, she felt impressed that marrying Jim was right and that things would work out. "The Lord had told me on my mission that I would marry Jim Kirk, and we would have the blessings of the Church," she said. After many long nights of pouring out her soul to God, asking how and why and when, her answer was only, "He will join." Mary realized she was going to have to be patient "to see how his conversion story was going to come about."

With faith she married Jim in an outdoor Quaker ceremony on his farm. More than three hundred of their friends and relatives came for the wedding, though Jim's devout Quaker family was skeptical of Mary's new religious ties. Her family was more tolerant, though none of them understood how she could be so deluded.

There were no signs that Jim would be one of those quick and miraculous conversions. It was hard for Mary to consistently attend meetings when the farm was so far from the meetinghouse and she was traveling alone. She found herself missing meetings sometimes. Jim came with her occasionally, but "he found it hard to justify missing all the work on the farm that day. I stuck to my guns about observing the Sabbath."

Weeks stretched into months and then years as Mary waited on the Lord. She worked at her definition of a homemaker—"smiling, wise, radiant, hard-working, and faithful." But the Kirks faced difficulties making ends meet. They eventually sold the farm and all the machinery at auction and moved to a smaller place. They hoped to have children, but that blessing didn't come quickly. What did come amid the trials they faced was an easing of the tension between them about the gospel.

Little by little Jim's interest grew. And then after two and a half years of marriage Mary wrote in her journal: "Tonight at 7 P.M. my husband was baptized and confirmed a member of The Church of Jesus Christ of Latter-day Saints. What a tremendous blessing and joy it was. Exactly six years ago today I went to the Provo Temple for my own endowment. I have waited so long for this moment and prayed for its accomplishment. The Lord promised me that it would come to pass, but I didn't know when. I am so pleased it was so soon. We have been married just two years and a half, and Jim has been taught so quickly and so fully by the Spirit of the Lord. He has had his mind opened and his hunger for truth satisfied, and he has taken that first great step. And now we talk of temple marriage and of having our baby sealed to us and of the work and service and doing whatever the Lord calls us to do."

Call the Kirks he did. Jim was soon branch president, and Mary the Relief Society president. Their family grew, and their Church responsibilities grew, too. Jim was called to a stake presidency, and Mary served in every auxiliary—sometimes in several callings at once—from Sunday School to Primary, Young Women, and Relief Society. They built upon each other's faith "and found comfort and strength in their joint commitment to the Son of God."

> *Till we all come in the unity of the faith, and of the*
> *knowledge of the Son of God.*
> Ephesians 4:13

# IT ALL BEGAN WITH TEAKWOOD CHAIRS

Ng Kat Hing stood in the furniture store ready to receive customers. The group of Americans in dark suits caught his attention, but what really interested him was how they addressed him.

"Brother Ng," one of them said. When Ng looked puzzled, the man asked, "Do you not believe there is one Father in Heaven?"

Ng pondered the question as he considered the man who had posed it. His nametag identified him as President Heaton. When Ng nodded yes to the question, the president continued, "So we are brothers, and I will call you that."

Brothers. President. Ng was intrigued. "I was touched and I was moved," Ng explained. "In that moment, a little bit of the restored gospel was manifest to me. I wondered about it all that day and through the night. Four days later when the man called back to confirm the furniture order, I knew I wanted to know more."

Indeed there was more to learn. President Grant Heaton, the newly called president of the Southern Far East Mission head-quartered in Hong Kong, was happy to satisfy Ng's curiosity as well as order his teakwood furniture from him. Ng was soon a language teacher for a host of missionaries and a member of The Church of Jesus Christ of Latter-day Saints. His roles eventually included branch president, district president, stake president, stake patriarch, counselor to the mission president, and regional representative. He and his wife served a mission to the Taipei Taiwan Temple, and he was called as president of the Hong Kong Temple, which opened in May 1996. It all began with teakwood desks and chairs.

That first encounter with the mission president and the missionaries had started twenty-five-year-old Ng thinking. He had been raised with a yearning for truth instilled in him as a child by his grandmother. "I was looking for a God who was different from the one I'd been taught about while growing up," he explained. His grandmother, a practicing Buddhist, had begun attending Christian churches shortly before her death. He had accompanied her. "But the pastors and preachers at those meetings were difficult to approach, and they were more concerned with donations than answering my questions."

Then President Heaton asked Ng to help him find someone who could tutor the missionaries in Cantonese. Ng approached a few friends he considered well qualified for the job. But when they showed no interest, he suggested himself for the position. Ng was not without credentials himself. He had studied at the Pooi Sun English College and the World Electrical Engineering College. That the new post came with a lower salary than his sales position at the furniture store was not an obstacle. "I had learned the truth," he said. "That was a good deal, right? Nothing is more important than that."

His spiritual conversion came when he taught the missionaries basic Cantonese and they taught him the gospel. He worked with several teams of missionaries before hearing all the pre-scribed lessons. "It took quite a while, but by the time I was baptized all my questions were answered. I had a strong foundation and a strong testimony."

On 31 May 1956 Ng Kat Hing was baptized in the swimming-pool-turned-baptismal-font at the mission home, now the site of the Hong Kong Temple. He was one of the first in Hong Kong to join the Church.

Ng's testimony has made a difference in many lives. "My wife told me I was entirely different after joining the Church. My temper was smooth. I became a gentleman. The managing of my finances went better because I paid my tenth to the Lord. I didn't worry about food or shelter because I kept the commandments. A happy life followed."

The missionaries' talk of God first touched his heart. "From the beginning, I learned about our Father in Heaven and his son, Jesus Christ. The missionaries taught of our relationship to these beings. And they continually talked of being children of God."

Acknowledging that in Hong Kong there is much pressure and stress in life, Brother Ng said, "Everyone is working so hard for money. We often spend so much time worrying about temporal things. The gospel brings a balance."

That balance has been a hallmark of his home. He and his wife, Ng Pang Lai, established priorities in rearing their seven children. "We made time for our children, for each other, and for our Church callings." Brother Ng gained a testimony of serving the Lord wherever and whenever.

"People say they have no time, but that is just an excuse," said Brother Ng. "They have the time for the things that are important in their lives."

His focus is clear. "We are all brothers and sisters. We need to share that knowledge with others."

*Teach the children of men the things which I have put*
*into your hands by the power of my Spirit.*
Doctrine and Covenants 43:15

# SOMETHING CHANGED ROSA

Rosa lived alone in a small rented room in the pueblo of Tiquisante, Guatemala. Her next-door neighbor Jose had agreed to hear the lessons taught by the missionaries of The Church of Jesus Christ of Latter-day Saints. On their first visit to teach Jose, the sister missionaries found him waiting for them outside in his hammock. Two weeks later Jose was baptized. His first Sunday at church he was asked to greet all the members and visitors at the door. He was delighted with the assignment.

All the time he listened to the sisters he wished his good friend Rosa would hear the gospel message. The missionaries tried to teach Rosa, but she had too many doubts, too many questions about doctrines that were contrary to those she had been taught as a child.

After Jose's baptism the sisters offered to teach him and Rosa to read. In December 1992, the First Presidency had announced a churchwide gospel literacy effort that President Gordon B. Hinckley described as "a great project." He promised: "Its consequences will go on and on and be felt in the lives of generations yet to come. It is a program . . . designed to bring light into the lives of those who can neither read nor write." ("Ambitious to Do Good," *Ensign,* Mar. 1992, 6.)

So the sisters, on Wednesday and Sunday afternoons, began teaching Rosa and Jose from the Church's literacy manuals that used scriptures as the text. Rosa wore thick, black-rimmed glasses held together with yarn and an elastic strap stretched around her head. She took the classes seriously, preparing a place for her teacher to sit by spreading her few extra clothes on the hot cement floor. Jose offered his tutor his prized wooden chair. The two were willing and diligent students.

At the end of each lesson, the missionaries asked one of the two to pray. Sister Jana Seiter, one of the missionaries, wrote: "I wish you could hear them pray when they ask God to please help them to learn to read his holy word. They also pray for us, thanking God for our health, our safety, our testimonies, our love, and asking him to continue blessing us in our missionary work."

In the middle of the reading lessons, Rosa's attitude changed. One day she was reticent; the next day she was eager. Something had happened.

The night before, the missionaries had asked her again if she would like to take the discussions because they were so encouraged by Rosa's progress in learning to read. After the sisters left, Rosa went into her room to get ready for bed. She had felt such a good spirit when the missionaries were there. When they left, she felt as if the light in her heart had gone out. Then horrible blackness surrounded her, and her faith failed her. Rosa tried praying, but the peace she wanted so badly did not come. Then she saw the Church literacy manual and picked it up. As Rosa paged through the book and read what little she could, she felt a peace, a beautiful calm. She realized that the book contained the word of God. She knew it. Those simple, single-syllable words filled her soul.

"It is different now," wrote Sister Seiter. "There is no objection that the Book of Mormon is adding nor taking away from the Bible. Now there is no doctrinal dispute. Now there is no tension. There is only love, trust, and sisterhood."

*God gave them knowledge and skill in all learning.*
Daniel 1:17

# WHY NOT US?

Naji Al-Jezrawi lived in Baghdad with his wife, Nawal, and their three daughters. Naji, fluent in several languages, worked there for the United Nations. But the family was Christian in a Muslim world. When the Gulf War began in 1991, Naji and his family fled the country.

At first they intended to relocate in India. Many of his countryman had gone there. But a friend from Germany suggested, "Go to Spain. It is much better, because the Catholic Refugee Commission there is very active." The family went to Spain, not knowing then that their Heavenly Father was guiding them to his Church. Arriving in July 1991, Naji immediately applied through the Catholic Commission to emigrate to the United States. Two months later they were interviewed along with many other Iraqi families.

Though all the other Iraqi families were given permission to enter the United States, the Al-Jezrawi family was denied. Naji was stunned. Every applicant was allowed to appeal three times, and he immediately did so. Their first and second appeals were rejected with no explanation.

Naji and his family asked, "Why only us?" They applied again. During the four months they waited for the official, final decision, Naji was introduced to the Church in the community of Mosteles, a suburb of Madrid, Spain.

One day, Latter-day Saint missionaries were making street contacts near the train station. Naji asked the blond young man, obviously an American, for directions. Stumbling in his Spanish, the young man turned to his companion, and the two began to sort out an answer in English. Naji heard their English and immediately asked them in English why they were in Spain.

They replied that they were missionaries for The Church of Jesus Christ of Latter-day Saints, a Christian church. That appealed to him, and he asked to hear more. The elders gave him the first discussion and a Book of Mormon right there at the train station. They set up an appointment to meet with his family the next week.

Naji prepared his wife and children for the visit, and when the elders arrived he had read the book. The elders gave the family a second discussion and asked for a baptismal commitment. Naji and his family agreed. Elders from the mission office and sister missionaries taught this "golden" family. They spent time together playing games, eating dinner, and reading and talking about the gospel. The missionaries introduced the five to the English-speaking Madrid Fifth Ward.

The baptism date was set for 8 July 1992, Naji's birthday. But he retreated from the decision, suggesting a later date. "Once Elder Bay heard that, a drop of tears fell down from his eyes. I asked him what was the matter, and he said that every time a date is fixed for baptism, Satan interferes and creates problems to cancel the baptism." Naji responded, "I want to challenge Satan. We'll move the date up to July 3." They did, and the family was baptized on that date by the mission president.

Naji recalled: "We were the luckiest Iraqi family even if we had been left behind. Now we were members of his Church. So, definitely our third appeal would be approved." But it was denied.

"We didn't know what to say or how to explain it. We kept asking ourselves, if we are members of his Church, why doesn't Heavenly Father help us? Why did he help other Iraqi families who are not even members? Why? Why? But we got no answer.

"Thank God our faith kept strong and we kept praying in order to be close to him. Then we said, It seems our Heavenly Father doesn't want us to go to the States. Let us try Canada."

Again the family went through the process of applying and being interviewed with other Iraqi families. Again, all the families were approved—except the Al-Jezrawis. The Canadian authorities explained that because Naji had worked with the United Nations, he had to be interviewed by special security representatives. "Here we said it was enough! We can't bear it anymore! Why only us, but there was no answer." Their faith began to waver. "But thank God, two things kept us strong. First our background in Christianity and second, the support of the members of the Madrid Fifth Ward."

The Saints came out in force. Their letters, visits, encouragement, suggestions, and faith in the Lord supported the new converts. One brother wrote to Naji, saying, "Life is more like a game of ask and answer. We ask for inspiration and direction to know his will for us, and he answers, always. The answers sometimes come quickly and clear and are immediately comprehensive to us;

or they may come much slower or unexpectedly and in ways not apparent to our understanding."

This brother was inspired. They all were. Two months later Naji had a second interview with the Canadian embassy, and they promised an answer within six weeks.

"While we were waiting for the reply, unexpected developments confirmed to us, first, there is nothing impossible to our Heavenly Father. Second, his inspiration can come through others, and third, when the time is right, Heavenly Father opens all the doors."

In this case the Lord worked through the mission president and his wife, who had become close friends with the Al-Jezrawi family. President and Sister Nelson asked the Lord why this faithful family was facing such a struggle. Naji recorded: "Our Heavenly Father's reply came to them that there was a possibility for Naji's family to proceed to the States. When they asked how, they got an answer on the spot saying, through the United Nations, because I had service in that organization."

Immediately Sister Nelson called the United Nations headquarters in New York, who referred her to the United Nations in Geneva, who referred her to the United Nations High Commission for Refugees in Madrid. They were willing to help. First they needed a copy of the original papers. Upon review they discovered that the Catholic Commission had filled out the papers incorrectly. The papers stated that Naji had never received persecution and that the family was in no danger. "All this time my family and I were suffering for the mistakes of man," said Naji, "not Heavenly Father forgetting us."

The United Nations office asked the International Rescue Mission to reconsider the case, though rarely are such requests granted. The interviews that followed were encouraging, and then the International office asked for evidence of persecution. They wanted affidavits in writing from individuals who had witnessed the abuse.

Finding former associates seemed an insurmountable task. The family had been gone from Baghdad for more than two years.

Naji knew someone who could vouch for his case who was now serving in Somalia. He knew another in Prague. Sister Nelson made the contacts, and in less than an hour and after a host of phone calls, a fax came from Somalia.

One to go. Simply finding the telephone listing in Prague seemed impossible until Sister Nelson called the Church mission office there. They got her the number, and Naji's associate answered. But he was retired, and the commission would accept only letters on official stationery. After many more phone calls explaining the problem, Sister Nelson arranged for the associate in Prague to take his statement to the American embassy. They attached it to their official stationery and faxed it on. The packet was complete. At last everything could be forwarded to the International office in Rome.

Within the next few days, visas came from Canada with a deadline attached. Naji was faced with making a decision without hearing if America was an option. He fasted and prayed. Would Heavenly Father want him to spend twenty-five hundred dollars for tickets to Canada if entry to America was an option? Out of time, Naji bought the tickets.

Late that evening news came from Rome: America had accepted the Al-Jezrawi family.

Recalled Naji: "It was such a joy to see the relief and excitement that we had after waiting for two years and three months. We cried from our happiness and kept asking, Do we deserve such blessings from our Heavenly Father? How easy he opened the doors to us and how he guided us to our ultimate goal. Whatever I do I will not be able to repay him for what he did for us. But I promise, and it is a promise, that I will serve his Church and his gospel with my utmost ability."

> *Be thou humble; and the Lord thy God shall lead thee*
> *by the hand, and give thee answer to thy prayers.*
> Doctrine and Covenants 112:10

# WAITING ON THE LORD

The story has been the same in so many countries. The gospel is planted in the hearts of those prepared. They wait weeks, months, even years, to be baptized and to see the Church established in their homelands. For Cyril West and his family, natives of Pakistan, it took nearly a decade.

In 1983 the Wests attended a meeting of the Latter-day Saints at the home of Church member Max Williams in Lahore, Pakistan, a meeting described by those present as "impressive" and "peaceful."

The Wests were converted by the love of Christ shown by the members. "This love was converted into a regular association with those families while we attended the Church meetings weekly for nearly five years. During this time our family became quite strong in church studies. Our meetings, which were like sacrament meetings, had between twenty and twenty-five people attending. Visitors came frequently, even Muslim visitors. I was most impressed by the teaching about free agency to choose the right way to live. Several times Brother Williams assured us that one day The Church of Jesus Christ of Latter-day Saints would be established in Pakistan. Knowing that gave us harmony and made us realize the importance of being obedient and worthy to be members."

Obedience became an important principle to the West family in the years ahead. Cyril wrote the *Church News* to ask that his story be published so that Church authorities would send someone to baptize him and his family. Elder Jack H. Goaslind, then a counselor in the International Mission, responded, urging Cyril and his family to continue their studies and meetings and to be patient. The Church would someday be established in Pakistan.

In the meantime, the investigators and the members continued to meet. Their number was sometimes increased by Church members from United States government agencies assigned to

Pakistan. Then they heard of the appointment of Niels Martin as branch president in Islamabad.

Cyril wasted no time in getting in touch with President Martin. His plea was simple: "We want to join." President Martin sent his two counselors, Brothers Douglas Bradford and Robert Simmons, to Lahore to baptize those patient investigators. Cyril and his wife, their daughter Loreen and sons Jerry and Anil; Cyril's father, Samuel; and Cyril's brother Earl and Earl's wife Virginia were all baptized.

Six months later the Saints in Lahore went to hear Elders John Carmack and Monte Brough from the Area Presidency speak at a meeting in Islamabad. The trip took them fourteen hours round trip in a public van. Brother West was firm: "We felt very blessed to be in the presence of such great men."

In July a missionary couple was assigned to help the dozen Saints in Lahore. On 2 October 1992 the Lahore Branch was organized under the direction of the Singapore Mission president and with the assistance of the Islamabad Branch presidency. Cyril West was called as branch president.

The Church had a place in the hearts and homeland of these believers.

> *Establish my word; yet ye shall be patient in long-*
> *suffering and afflictions, that ye may show*
> *forth good examples unto them in me, and*
> *I will make an instrument of thee in my*
> *hands unto the salvation of many souls.*
> Alma 17:11

# "NOTICE TO JAPANESE SAINTS"

On 6 April 1924 mission president Hilton A. Robertson performed the first marriage of a Latter-day Saint in Japan. The marriage of Church member Fujiya Nara to Motoko Yoshimizu seemed to signal the beginning of a great era for the Land of the

Rising Sun and The Church of Jesus Christ of Latter-day Saints. But it was not to be. Not yet.

Fujiya Nara had begun attending Sunday School in the Sapporo Branch at age thirteen. For four years he studied the Book of Mormon and Church history. He was baptized in Tokyo by mission president Joseph H. Stimpson on 6 July 1915. Active in the Church's Mutual Improvement Association (MIA) and devoted to his new religion, he was ordained an elder in 1923, the first native Japanese to hold that priesthood office.

But on 31 July 1924, only three months after Fujiya's marriage, the Church closed the mission in Japan. Little success and declining American-Japanese relations prompted the removal of the missionaries after twenty-three years. The Japanese Saints were left without the mission program but not without hope. Fujiya stepped forward to unify and bolster the faith of his fellow Saints. There were 137 members.

Fujiya prepared a flyer to organize the MIA. In his bulletin, published under the title "Shuro," he heralded the MIA efforts as "the path to light in the present darkness." Shuro, a Japanese reference to the palm leaves used to herald Jesus' triumphal entry into Jerusalem before his crucifixion, was distributed to all the Church members Brother Nara could find. Having served as the clerk in the Tokyo Office, he had record and membership lists from which to draw. For two years his efforts kept the members in contact. Then in 1926 the Church established MIA organizations in Sapporo, Osaka, and Tokyo, and Brother Nara was called to preside over the units and represent the Church on a limited scale.

Brother Nara did all he could. Then in 1933 his employment took him to Manchuria, and he lost contact with other Japanese Saints and Church headquarters until after World War II. Back in Tokyo and struggling with the devastation of war, Brother Nara's hopes for regular Church affiliation were rekindled by a small advertisement in the 30 October 1945 newspaper—a "Notice to Japanese Latter-day Saints."

Brother Nara was grateful for that day. Years later he recalled,

"I had no doubt that such a time would surely come if we kept following the commandments and praying without losing hope."

Church member Edward Clissold, a United States naval officer with the American forces occupying Japan, had placed the ad in hopes of rallying any Japanese Saints, who had now been without formal Church leadership for more than twenty years.

Brother Nara quickly contacted Brother Clissold and again began searching for members, hoping for the return of missionaries. He brought together a small group of remaining Japanese Saints, and in less than two years, on 6 March 1948, the Japanese Mission was reorganized under President Clissold.

Church services soon included two Sunday School classes. Fifty-two attended one class at Brother Nara's home, and forty-three attended another in the home of a nonmember.

Brother Nara also had prepared a convert for baptism. His wife, Motoko, was baptized by President Clissold a month after the mission reopened.

Brother Nara's missionary service had just begun. At the time of his death in July 1992, there were approximately ninety-six thousand members of the Church in Japan. He had played a prominent role in that gathering, serving his God and his people in various callings from priest to branch president to patriarch of the Japan Tokyo North Stake.

> *They were firm, and steadfast, and immovable,*
> *willing with all diligence to keep the*
> *commandments of the Lord.*
> 3 Nephi 6:14

---

# A PROMISE OF TEMPLE BLESSINGS

Johann Denndorfer's visit to the Swiss Temple in January 1974 was the end of a long and devoted journey. A member of The Church of Jesus Christ of Latter-day Saints since 1913, he had

been imprisoned for his beliefs, his Church books had been confiscated, and his requests for a visa to visit the temple had been
rejected time after time by the Communist government of his
native Hungary. He had collected his own tithing in a special
account, hoping some day to turn it over to a proper Church
authority. Through the persecution and the isolation, he had
remained faithful to the covenants he made at baptism.

Then, at age eighty-one, he received his own endowment,
was sealed to his wife, and did the temple work for many of his
ancestors. He had been blessed.

Johann's life had been one of commitment and endurance.
And life had been hard. He remembered the night when as a
young man he had been arrested and thrown in jail and then ban-
ished from Germany for preaching. That was 1913, and Europe
hovered on the brink of war. A small group of Saints were meeting weekly to discuss the Bible, and Johann, then working in a
coal mine, had joined their group. One night he had been asked
to fill in for the regular teacher who had been detained at work.
A new convert, Johann was uncertain of his ability to lead the discussion and suggested others were more qualified. But he was
chosen, and with a faint heart he did his best.

The group was supportive and friendly. They viewed being
together as Saints as an important part of their lives. At the end
of the lively discussion, the song, and the prayer, Johann and one
of the sisters began closing up the meeting place to go home
when a hand reached out and gripped Johann's arm. "In the name
of the law," the heavy Prussian voice said, "you are under arrest."

Johann spent the night in jail. The Prussian police had falsely
identified him as an American missionary. That he was from
Hungary (then Transylvania) was his good fortune: he was not
prosecuted but simply deported. As he waited for the police to
take action, he pondered what had happened to him since he had
joined the LDS Church. He hadn't been seeking religion when he
came to Germany but had been introduced to the gospel by his
landlords. They had answers to questions that had always

troubled him. And now he was losing his job and being expelled from Germany.

Soberly, he recognized that perhaps the hand of God was in the situation. The other men at the meeting were native Germans; they had families to support and needed their jobs. He was a foreigner, single, and better able to rebound. His spirits lifted, and he found himself sharing his testimony with the jailer, who, impressed by his sincerity and sense of purpose, warned others in the cell not to harm him.

Johann was deported to Switzerland, where he immediately contacted the mission president and began assisting the missionaries by passing out tracts and bearing his testimony. He was soon ordained a deacon. He later described this period as "the most wonderful time of my life."

He didn't stay long in Switzerland and soon returned to Hungary and his family. There he enlisted in the military and was sent to the Russian front. War took its toll, and Johann was wounded. He spent eleven months in a Budapest hospital.

The Communist takeover of Hungary stranded Johann for forty years. He was separated from most Church members and from Church meetings. He kept up correspondence with his Church friends in Switzerland and Germany, subscribed to the Church's German publication, *Der Stern,* and studied the scriptures. Most important, Johann kept in touch with God.

He married and reared a family, moved several times, and changed jobs, but he stayed faithful to his beliefs.

In 1955 at age sixty-one Johann was ordained an elder. President Herold Gregory of the German mission sent Elder Richard Ranglack to Hungary to interview Johann and give him the Melchizedek Priesthood.

The Lord soon gave him an opportunity to use his priesthood. A sister whom he called on as a home teacher turned to him for a blessing. She was suffering from a high fever that had exhausted her. They prayed together and then he left, promising to return with consecrated oil to give her a blessing. He described the experience:

"It was my first opportunity to use the power of God. Just imagine, in the scriptures it says for us to call upon the elders, but I was alone. From that time on I began to fast, went upon my knees, and asked the Lord for his support in my fear and trembling. . . .

"During the night I didn't sleep much, but prayed a lot. . . . The next morning I tried to buy olive oil, but finding none, I got some cooking oil. In the afternoon when I went to visit Sister Toth again, she still had a high fever. I anointed her and then in a little while sealed the anointing on her head. I then read out of the Doctrine and Covenants about blessing the sick; when I looked over, she had fallen asleep. I felt her hand; the fever seemed to have lessened. I asked her mother-in-law to let her sleep until she woke, and then left the apartment.

"To my amazement, I found her [two days later] out by the front gate looking into the street. I asked her how she was and she said she had been able to get out of bed the day before. She said it was very good that I had come, because she had already been in bed for over a week."

At one point, Johann was accused by the Hungarian secret police of being an "American spy," and his Church materials so carefully kept for many years were seized. He was crushed but remained faithful. He applied for a visa to visit East Germany where he knew Saints were joining in a conference. His application was denied, and his subsequent applications were dismissed as well.

His health began to fail, yet he held out hope that he would be reunited with a body of Saints. His chances dimmed when he was admitted to the hospital with a serious liver ailment and skin disease that kept him there for more than a month.

This time his home teacher, Walter Krause, patriarch for many years behind the Iron Curtain, gave him a patriarchal blessing.

Brother Krause, who with his wife, Edith, lived in Dresden, East Germany, had been Johann's lifeline to the Church for years. Brother Krause and his wife were Johann's home teachers, traveling to Hungary at least once a year for a visit. President Thomas S. Monson has told the story of Brother Kraus calling a young companion and asking, "Would you like to go with me to do some home teaching?" The young man said he would and then asked, "Where are we going?" Brother Krause replied, "Hungary." And off they went to visit Johann Denndorfer.

One of the first patriarchal blessings Brother Krause ever gave—among the 1,650 blessings to members behind the Iron Curtain—was to Johann. Brother Krause promised Johann that he would go to the temple. Still, health, age, and government restrictions seemed to stand in the way—not to mention that he had no way to do his family history research because getting out of Hungary was impossible for him. So, Sister Kraus researched his family lines back ten generations and cleared 1,420 names for temple work.

Brother Denndorfer continued to apply for permission to go to Switzerland. He was refused, again and again. Brother Krause encouraged him to try one more time.

This time permission came. Johann's passport was approved, and he was allowed to travel to Switzerland, where he was going not to a conference but to the temple. There he spent two weeks doing work for the family members whose names Sister Kraus had helped him find. At the end of those two weeks, he sent the rest of the names to the Freiberg Germany Temple where his fellow Saints finished the work he had started.

*I have fought a good fight, I have finished*
*my course, I have kept the faith.*
2 Timothy 4:7

# TENDER APPLES

Whang Kuen-Ok always wanted to do something for God. Reared a devout Presbyterian on a farm in Japanese-occupied Korea before World War II, she prayed as a child for the opportunity to go to school so that she could devote her efforts to God.

Recognizing the lack of health care for her people, she hoped to study medicine. But Korean society viewed women as having a subordinate role and medical training seemed out of reach.

But her prayers were answered when an opportunity came for her to attend junior high school. There she distinguished herself as an honor student while working to pay her school expenses. Her performance qualified her to apply to nursing school.

But the same passion that she applied to her studies caused her to be expelled from school for her refusal to worship the Japanese emperor. It was a difficult time in Korea. Poverty plagued the country; people everywhere were suffering.

When the Allied Forces liberated Korea on 15 August 1945, she described the momentous occasion this way: "Every creature, even trees and mountains, seemed to joy for the freedom that we had fought for a long time." Whang and many of her friends determined to lift those so ravaged by persecution and war, children in particular. But the joy was short-lived as the Communists divided the country. Whang escaped to the south "just as the fences went up between what would be North and South Korea." She left behind her family and her childhood friends.

Immediately she began working in refugee camps, trying to make a difference amid cold, hunger, anger, and disappointment. She continued to pray for her "solemn mission." She said, "I knew I wanted to help as many poor people as possible, even though I didn't think I had the ability, skill, or power. In order to do that, I knew that I would have to sacrifice worldly possessions, and I knew that I must always fortify myself spiritually."

For six years teaching in the camps was both her vocation

and her avocation. In November 1958, prompted by her minister, she was accepted to an exchange program at the University of California at Berkeley. Arriving at the campus, she soon developed a friendship with two other Korean students from Brigham Young University who were spending the summer at Berkeley. Less than a year later she visited BYU and fell in love with the mountains. The faith of the Latter-day Saint students touched her soul; she felt comfortable with them.

For the next three years she studied social work at BYU, returning to Korea in 1962. In her homeland she asked for the missionary discussions and joined the Church.

Her next years were successful. She ran an orphanage. In the process she brought attention to the plight of the children and built support for their cause. She did it with dignity, dedication, and grace. An American serviceman helped her launch a highly successful effort to create a children's choir, and he marveled at the magic she brought to what would otherwise have been a bleak setting. But when the owners of her school learned she was a Latter-day Saint, they demanded she convert to their religion or be dismissed.

Sister Whang resolved the problem quickly. She started an orphanage of her own where she was free to teach gospel principles, hold family home evening, and acquaint the children with Jesus Christ. The Tender Apples Home started each morning with hymn singing, prayer, and scripture study at 6 A.M. Sister Whang was up before the girls so that she could pray and study the scriptures on her own, stoke the fires, and set things in order.

Korean Mission President Eugene Till paid tribute to Sister Whang: "She would tell you what she needed, and she would accept nothing less than total fulfillment. She never took her eye off a goal until it was accomplished. You can understand that kind of determination when a person is going to gain something from her work. But when the results of Sister Whang's efforts came— clothing, money, food—she didn't keep any of it for herself."

Her girls were influential in spreading the gospel. A singing group of elders from the mission and the Tender Apples Choir performed frequently, raising awareness of the Church's name throughout the country.

Sister Whang served as a district and stake Relief Society president and as a temple worker in the Seoul Korea Temple from its opening in 1985. Typical of her dedication, she worked two days a week in the temple instead of the usual one.

Sister Whang placed many of her girls with Latter-day Saint families. Over a period of twenty years she cared for eighty-four children. Many went to live with LDS families in the United States. Twelve were married in the temple; nine served full-time missions. Her life was a mission of its own.

*As for me and my house, we will serve the Lord.*
Joshua 24:15

# THEY BROKE DOWN AND CRIED

In 1994, disaster struck the southern United States. Rains, hurricanes, and floods pounded one community after another. In a particularly hard-hit area, the stake Relief Society president was asked to assess the damage done to homes in her stake. Every home she visited was badly damaged. She went into one kitchen, sloshing through mud above her ankles, and opened a cupboard to see if any dishes or food supplies had survived the flooding. Inside was coiled a water moccasin snake. She quickly shut the door and tried another cupboard, where she came eye-to-eye with yet another snake. In consternation she ran up the stairs to the second floor. There she encountered an alligator!

The Chattanooga Tennessee Stake decided to cancel the annual Pioneer Day celebrations to help their neighbors in Georgia clean up. One group was assigned to an area where the homes had been covered with water. They were to help owners get their houses prepared for reconstruction.

On July 17 a crew of fifteen finished stripping one home back to the plasterboard on the walls and moved to the next one on the block. Danny Wolfe, a volunteer from the stake, described the scene: "The owner had been working with his two friends when we arrived. You can imagine the relief of seeing fifteen men pull up with eight wheelbarrows, shovels, hammers, and other tools. We went right to work. The Lord blessed us. As we finished, one member of our group overheard the owner saying to his friend, 'I can't believe it. They have accomplished more in one hour than we accomplished in three days.'"

Jane and Mike McDonald, a young couple in Leesburg, wrote a letter of thanks to the members of the Chattanooga stake. "We want to thank you and your crew so much for the help you gave us in clearing out our house after the flood. You saved my husband and me many hours of work. We will always remember your help."

The McDonalds weren't members of the Church. When the workers from the Chattanooga stake finished cleaning out the McDonalds' house, one of the brethren, not knowing the family was of another religion and trying to encourage them, asked if they had been to the temple yet. They responded, "No, we are not members of your faith." The brother just put his arms around the man's shoulder and asked him to consider learning more about the LDS Church. Wrote the stake president: "A wonderful feeling of brotherhood prevailed in those few moments together. No promises were made, but these brethren on the work crew knew they had left a favorable impression upon the souls of this young couple."

Rick Youngblood of the Hixson Tennessee Ward related his experience in helping clean up: "During our visit on the first weekend we went to Albany, our group was preparing to leave after a full day's work. The tools and crews were loaded in the trucks, and the workers were tired and hungry. As we were preparing to leave, it came to my attention that a retired widower was struggling to recover from his entire home being destroyed. He was extremely distraught and confused about where to begin."

Brother Youngblood described the scene: "Our group knew that this nonmember needed help. The first few men in the home found him sitting in the main room crying. Shovels, rakes, hammers, brooms, wheelbarrows were unloaded and with tools in hand about thirty men converged upon the house. The change in the brother's countenance was incredible. Where a few minutes before he had been despondent, he was now excited and rejuvenated. In about thirty minutes, the inside of the home was completely gutted down to the stud walls. As the last wheelbarrow was loaded into the truck, the last thank-you's graciously expressed, a feeling of great joy and satisfaction settled into the hearts of those who were there."

The flooding was particularly devastating in the city of Albany and its surrounding area. Some twenty-three square miles were under water, and more than a third of the residents were without homes and food.

Coordinating some of the flood relief efforts was Ritchey M. Marbury, who described just one of many miracles: "As soon as I recognized there was going to be an immediate need for food, clothing, and cleaning supplies, I contacted the bishops storehouse in Atlanta, Georgia. Within five hours a tractor trailer loaded with every requested item pulled into the parking lot of the LDS church.

"The next day I was attending a county commission meeting in Lee County when they spoke of a severe shortage of food and supplies there. The pastor of the Leesburg United Methodist Church indicated they were serving as a storehouse for food and clothing. Lee Country was not yet receiving help from any of the other agencies and was in desperate need of additional food."

A forty-eight-foot tractor trailer leaving the Albany bishops storehouse was sent to the Leesburg Methodist church. The trailer arrived fifteen minutes after all available food supplies had been given out. Some of the Methodist church members reported that when they saw this huge truck loaded with food and other supplies coming from the LDS Church and arriving in their parking lot, they simply broke down and cried.

*They did walk uprightly before God, imparting to one*
*another both temporally and spiritually*
*according to their needs.*
Mosiah 18:29

# COME, LISTEN TO A PROPHET'S VOICE

More than fifty people stood in the Tahiti Papeete Mission office. They had come to see the prophet, Spencer W. Kimball, who was holding an area conference for the members in this part of French Polynesia.

The mission president looked at the crowd gathered around him. Not recognizing a single face, he assumed they were nonmembers interested in attending the conference.

He was stunned when they introduced themselves. They were members of the Church from the tiny island of Taenga, located in the Tuamotu Archipelago. He quickly learned that nearly all the people on the island were members of the Church, and they had made the three-day voyage in a schooner to be with their prophet and Church leader.

It was a surprise to hear there were members of the Church on the island, but to hear that all but a few of the seventy-six residents were Latter-day Saints was incredible news. Somehow in the transmission of mission and Church records through World War II, the entire "island" had been misplaced. But communication from Church leaders in Tahiti had always been difficult at best. There are 110 islands in French Polynesia, scattered over more than a million square miles of the Pacific Ocean.

That Church membership records had been lost was a startling realization. That the members weren't lost at all was a testimony of their faith to carry on. Somehow, Taenga had been missed as the Latter-day Saint stronghold it was.

Taenga, an atoll about four hundred miles east of Tahiti, had limited communication with other islands. There was no airstrip. The route to get there entailed flying to Makemo on a small plane and then traveling by motorboat at least three hours on the open sea. If weather is bad, the boat ride can take six hours. But the island boasts solar-generated power for every household, one of the few modern additions to a fairly simple style of life.

In 1844 when the Prophet Joseph Smith dispatched missionaries to the Sandwich Islands, they ended up in what is now known as French Polynesia. It is recognized as the first foreign-speaking mission of the Church. The early missionaries had success. Benjamin Grouard landed on the island of Tuamotus and in May 1845 went to Anaa, an island not far from the small island of Taenga. He baptized more than six hundred people in five months and organized several branches.

In 1852 the missionaries were expelled by the French government, and for twenty years no elders were allowed to proselyte in the area. It was another twenty years before any missionaries were assigned to the islands, but the members carried the gospel message to their friends and neighbors on surrounding islands. Many were converted, including residents of Taenga. Though official contact with the Church leaders in Tahiti was erratic, Taenga's members continued faithful.

In 1931 the Church had acquired a forty-foot-by-forty-five-foot tract of land on Taenga for a chapel. Since that time, the twenty-foot-by-thirty-foot building had helped keep the members strong. They remembered the last official visit by a mission president to have been in the late 1950s.

Though the Saints in Taenga had not been in contact with Church officials, they knew they had a prophet of God and they had come to see him. Their faith was strong and their commitment to God vibrant.

"We always lived the gospel as best we could," said Sister Teuruhai Buchin, who later worked in the Papeete Tahiti Temple.

So sure were the islanders of their place in the kingdom of God that one of them, Kaheke Temanu, built a small residence to be used exclusively by the mission president should he come to visit the island. Brother Temanu was later called as the island's branch president.

Somehow these steadfast members learned by word of mouth that the prophet of the Lord was coming to Tahiti. Three prophets—David O. McKay, Joseph Fielding Smith, and Harold B. Lee—had served since the islanders had had any official contact with the Church. They brought with them handcrafted gifts for their prophet.

And they received a gift in return. President Kimball spoke of gathering as a people: "The Saints were driven across the country to the Salt Lake Valley, which was a dry, forbidding country. Since that time, the members of the Church from all lands have been rushing to Salt Lake City. For many years there has been the cry, 'Come to Zion, Come to Zion!' But the last few years we have been saying to the Saints, 'Stay in Zion, for Zion is wherever you are.'" (In Tahiti Area Conference Report, Mar. 1976, 36.)

> *Wherefore, we search the prophets, and we have many*
> *revelations and the spirit of prophecy; and having*
> *all these witnesses we obtain a hope, and our*
> *faith becometh unshaken, insomuch that we*
> *truly can command in the name of Jesus*
> *and the very trees obey us, or the*
> *mountains, or the waves*
> *of the sea.*
> Jacob 4:6

# FILLING IN THE FOOTINGS

When the pioneers arrived in the Salt Lake Valley, they immediately began building Zion. Said Brigham Young, "This is a good place to make Saints." (*Journal of Discourses*, 4:32.) Cabins, meetinghouses, and other buildings went up in a hurry to house the rapidly expanding Church. Today, building Zion in countries around the world has required permits and permissions and given plenty of opportunity for opposition.

The construction of the first chapel in Hungary faced such problems. Just as the nineteenth-century Church pioneers had encountered mobs who tarred and feathered them to discourage their religious activity, so in the early 1990s the Hungarian Saints faced closed doors, bureaucratic red tape, and philosophical collapse. Confusion reigned.

In 1993 Hanno Luschin, area architect for the Church in Europe, visited Szombathely, Hungary, to look at a possible location for a chapel. He well knew the process of working with government entities, having directed the building of the Freiberg Germany Temple and several chapels in Europe, including Russia.

The local architect drove with Brother Luschin the three hours from Budapest to the community whose growing branch activity could support a new chapel. "We arrived in the city and tried to locate the proposed site," Brother Luschin remembered. "On the way there, we drove by a piece of property that caught my attention.

"'Now that looks like a good place to build a church!' I said. But it was not the site that had been selected, and we drove on, finally stopping at a different lot."

When the two began to walk the ground, "I could not help but feel disappointment," Brother Luschin recalled. "I had felt so much better about the other location."

But the city officials were firm in their decision that this was the only available land, and so the Church proceeded. The plans were drawn up, and construction began that fall. The site was excavated, and the concrete footings poured.

When word came from Hungarian officials that "we were to stop construction because there were objections from a local church whose cemetery was located close by," Brother Luschin was not surprised. He had had plenty of firsthand experience with disappointments and delays.

What happened next was reminiscent of the experience of the early Saints, who had buried the newly completed foundation of the Salt Lake Temple just before the arrival of Johnston's Army in 1858. In Hungary, Brother Luschin's workers covered the concrete footings with soil and abandoned the project.

Brother Luschin had encountered similar difficulties only three years before in Vyborg, Russia, where he had gone in 1990 to purchase property to build the first Latter-day Saint meetinghouse in that country. "Finding a piece of property suitable for the construction of a meetinghouse proved to be a most humbling experience, one far more difficult than I had ever imagined," Brother Luschin recalled. Despite the easing of government restrictions and the dramatic shift to a more open economy, Brother Luschin was told by officials, "Russian land is not for sale. It belongs to all the people of Russia." The collapse of Communism had not reshaped everyone's thinking. Nevertheless, after countless negotiations over many months, the Church was able to lease some property, and a ground-breaking ceremony was set. On the morning that Presiding Bishop Merrill Bateman and local priesthood leaders had planned to conduct the ceremony, the lease was rescinded by officials. It was 1996 before an LDS chapel in Vyborg was built and dedicated.

In Hungary, Brother Luschin saw the difficulty of finding property being repeated. He began the search for a new site by suggesting the property he had been drawn to when he first entered the city a year before. Permission eventually was granted to purchase that land. Construction began again, and in November 1995 the Szombathely Chapel, the first meetinghouse built by the Church in Hungary, was dedicated.

*For it must needs be, that there is an*
*opposition in all things.*
2 Nephi 2:11

# HUMILITY AND OBEDIENCE

The pioneers struggled and suffered on the plains, and they continued to be tested as they began to build Zion. To their faith and dedication, they added the power that humility and obedience brought to their lives.

Pioneer Ephraim Hanks was at work one morning building an adobe house in Salt Lake City. The basement was nearly completed and he was preparing to lay the sun-dried brick when Brigham Young drove up in his carriage. "Ephraim, how thick is that rock wall?" he asked.

Ephraim answered, "Eight inches." Said President Young, "Tear it all down and build it twice as thick." For several days Ephraim had hauled the rock from Ensign Peak. He had paid a mason a good price to lay it in lime mortar. Now, Brigham Young was advising him to do it again.

The mason spoke up, "Brigham Young may be a saint, but he's no kind of prophet about building stone walls." Hanks nevertheless set about to double the walls of his home.

A month later a storm raged through the area, just as they completed the sixteen-inch wall. Rain fell in torrents, flooding the basement of the new home. But the thick walls stood firm. When the water drained, Hanks finished placing the rafters of his sturdy home, one he knew would shelter his family for many years.

Modern-day pioneers have found that humility and obedience

are essential to building homes that will withstand the storms of latter-day secularism.

---

# THREE SACKS OF POTATOES

Phebe and Parley P. Pratt and Rufus C. Allen were the first Latter-day Saint missionaries to Chile, in 1851, but the language barrier and civil disturbances stymied their five-month missionary effort. More than a century later, on 23 June 1956, LDS missionary work began again. This time the results have been phenomenal. Chile now has more than seventy stakes, six missions, a temple, and its own Area Presidency.

Large congregations are one measure of Zion's growth in Chile, but the real strength of the gospel lies in the hearts and testimonies of the individual members. Jose and Juana Yefi are a prime example. The Yefis live in the Estacion Ward of the Puerto Montt Stake, but for them to get to church they have to ride two hours by horse, three hours by boat, and another hour and a half by bus. Each way.

The Yefi parents and their seven children live in the remote mountain valley of El Callao. Thick forests of coigue, laurel, tepu, and ulmo trees separate them from the bustle of the nearest city, Puerto Varas. But they are certainly not alone. They are united in their goal, displayed on a plaque in the dining room, "To Build an Eternal Family."

No missionaries knocked on their door to introduce them to the gospel. Jose Yefi had gone to see a doctor in Puerto Varas to get treatment for serious nosebleeds he had suffered since childhood—some so severe that he fainted. Those recurrent nosebleeds led to his conversion.

"I was at a friend's house. He told me that two young men lived nearby who 'cured' people in the name of the Lord. Since I have always been a faithful man, I went to see them and asked them how much they charged for a blessing. The young men, who stood out because of their white shirts, told me, 'We don't charge money to bless one of our brethren. If you have faith that you will be healed with the blessing we give you, it will be the Lord who will really cure you.'

"Then they invited me to sit down, but I told them, 'I don't feel comfortable when I'm sitting down. I would feel better kneeling.' The missionaries put their hands on my head and gave me a blessing. The experience was marvelous. I felt warm all over my body, and I had no doubt that it was God's power curing me. Never again did I have a nosebleed.

"After this experience, I asked the missionaries what I had to do to become a member of their church. They asked me if I was married. I told them, yes, and we made an appointment to meet together with my wife the following Sunday. The missionaries presented the first discussion. They asked us to return the next week for the second discussion, but I told them that because of the distance involved, I wanted them to baptize us then. So we received all the discussions and were baptized the same day, September 28, 1979."

The Yefi family was dedicated to the Lord and his Church. The long distance between their home and the nearest congregation made attendance difficult, but they went as often as possible. On one of those visits Brother Yefi was ordained to the Aaronic Priesthood.

At that time, Julio Otay was the branch president in Puerto Varas. He challenged Brother Yefi to increase his commitment to the Lord and the gospel by paying his tithing and by preparing himself to receive the Melchizedek Priesthood.

Jose Yefi committed to do what he was asked. Not many months passed before he appeared at the branch president's office. It was a rainy, cold day, not particularly good traveling weather, and Brother Yefi, undeterred by the constant drizzle, was soaked. He asked to speak with President Otay about his tithing outside. There, propped against the building, were three sacks of potatoes. He had brought them by horseback, boat, and bus to be given to the Lord.

In Brother Yefi's determination to do all that the Lord has asked, he has become a remarkable missionary. His father, his brother, his brother's wife, and one of their daughters, his brother-in-law and his wife, their oldest son, and two younger daughters have been drawn to the Church by the Yefi family's example. All were taught the gospel by Brother Yefi before they made the trip to Puerto Varas to be interviewed by the full-time missionaries so Brother Yefi could baptize them.

The Yefis have been sealed in the Santiago Temple, and they testify to their fellow Church members of that wonderful opportunity.

Every Sunday in that remote mountain hamlet, eighteen faithful Saints gather. Occasionally others who have been touched by the pioneer spirit of this remarkable family meet with them. Their priesthood leaders have authorized them to hold Church services in the Yefis' modest front room.

When Brother Yefi was baptized, he and his family struggled to survive on very little—a team of oxen that he used to plow his fields, a horse, and several goats and sheep. But times have changed. Brother Yefi explains: "We have been greatly blessed. I have horses, goats, sheep and nine milking cows that give us enough milk to feed our children and to make cheese to sell. And we sow and harvest our own wheat. We are very blessed."

Says Church leader Benigno Pantoja, who served as regional representative in that area and visited the Yefis in their home, "As I told the Yefi family good-by, I thought about the lessons I had learned from them. I learned about being faithful to the Lord in every circumstance. I learned that although a great distance separated the Yefis from the church meetinghouse, there was no distance between them and the Lord."

> *Hath not God chosen the poor of this world rich in faith,*
> *and heirs of the kingdom which he hath*
> *promised to them that love him?*
> James 2:5

# I SANG TO MYSELF

Robert Israel Muhile was one of the first from Tanzania to accept the gospel. He was converted while working and studying in Cairo, Egypt. He observed that the couple who taught him the gospel were "very kind people. I liked them so much, they made me want to change my life." And he did. His decision to join the Church brought him "great joy and peace."

A year later Robert, by then an elder, returned to his home in Tanzania with the strong desire to convert his family. Like so many of the early pioneers who were disappointed in their efforts to share the truth with their families, he was unsuccessful. His family had no interest in his newfound religion. He was isolated from other Church members, for his home in Dar es Salaam was six hundred miles, three days by bus, from the nearest branch of the Church.

Seeking spiritual guidance, wanting to recommit to his baptismal covenants and share in the blessings of partaking of the sacrament, Robert went to the mission president Larry Brown in Nairobi, Kenya, and requested permission to administer the sacrament to himself each Sunday. His plea was granted.

Again in Dar es Salaam, Robert invited his family to come to his worship service. They declined, and so he held his meeting alone. He describes how he conducted these poignantly solitary Sunday meetings:

"I prepared water and bread. I also had more water to clean my hands and a small towel. I sang a song to myself out loud. I had my hymn book. After that I offered an opening prayer. Because I was alone, I didn't have any business to do, so I sang the sacrament hymn and prepared the sacrament. Then I knelt and blessed it and took it. After the sacrament I covered it, as we respect it always. I offered myself a talk—my testimony. Then I sang as we did in Sunday School and then read from *Gospel Principles*. I finished with a prayer. I then attended priesthood meeting. After singing a hymn, I said a prayer and then read a lesson from the priesthood manual. After that, I finished by singing and then offered the closing prayer. Each Sunday I had all three meetings. When I partook of the emblems it helped me to be more worthy."

> Grace and peace be multiplied unto you . . . through
> the knowledge of him that hath called
> us to glory and virtue.
> 2 Peter 1:2–3

# THEY HAD COME SO FAR

When the small, sturdy passenger boat cast off from the pier at the Port of Manaus, Brazil, the 102 men, women, and children were prepared for the journey of a lifetime. From the heart of the Amazon rain forest to the São Paulo temple, these modern-day pioneers from the Manaus Stake, the fifty-seventh stake organized in Brazil, traveled the 3,890 miles by river and bus to reach the temple. The journey was not unlike that of the Saints who more than a hundred years before had crossed the Atlantic and then the barren plains of North America to join with fellow Saints in Zion. It would be a long six days and nights before the Saints of Manaus arrived at the temple. But as a people they had already come so far.

The Latter-day Saints in Brazil had rejoiced when President Spencer W. Kimball announced at the 1975 São Paulo Area Conference that a temple would be built in their homeland. For the 208,000 members in Brazil, the closest temple was in Washington, D.C., a distance that was prohibitive. It made sense that the first temple in South America would be built in São Paulo, Brazil, because that country had the greatest concentration of Church members. São Paulo itself had sixteen chapels, five stakes, thirty-six wards and branches, two missions, and most of the area offices for South America. The new temple would be the seventeenth working temple built by the Latter-day Saints.

During the three and a half years between the announcement of the temple and its dedication, the Saints had much to do. "We must awaken to the concept that after baptism there are many more steps to take," Elder William Grant Bangerter, area supervisor for Brazil, said in 1975 when the temple was first announced. "I think the desire is there among the faithful members of the Church, but it's a new teaching to them."

Church members from most of South America were included in the temple district, and they all sacrificed to assist in the construction. Leaders set goals to help the South American Saints understand temple work: at least two thousand prospective elders would be ordained to the Melchizedek Priesthood so that they could take their families to the temple; ten thousand would have temple recommends by the time the temple opened; and all members would try to prepare four-generation family group sheets. "If they're faithful in doing it," Elder Bangerter said at the time, "we'll have 100,000 names ready to present to the temple."

On 30 October 1978 the first latter-day house of the Lord in South America was dedicated. President Kimball asked the Lord in the dedicatory prayer, "May peace abide in all the homes of the Saints, may holy angels guard them."

The Church members from Manaus who were traveling to the São Paulo Brazil Temple in 1991 felt its power. The first leg of their journey was along the powerful Amazon River and its tributaries. An airplane trip from Manaus to São Paulo would have been much shorter—only 1,630 miles in a four-hour plane trip. But the fare was prohibitive, so the members journeyed by boat and bus.

The boat ride was at first joyful and relaxing as the members shared their hopes and dreams and excitement over visiting the house of the Lord, now less than a week away. They had the services of a cook, and despite cramped quarters, they all slept well on board the boat.

The third day on the river was the eighth birthday of one of the children. The boat stopped at Praia do Dourado ("Golden Beach") and, after checking the river for alligators and piranhas, the father baptized his daughter. The Saints decorated the boat with balloons in tribute to this significant event and the spiritual journey that began at baptism and was now reaching a new dimension.

On the fourth day they arrived in Humaita, their port of debarkation. Pouring rain drenched them as they transferred their bags from the boat to the bus that would carry them to the temple. The wearying part of the journey began, as the bus lumbered along the narrow country roads. That the next miles would be less than luxurious was obvious: there were no sleeping quarters, no showers, no cook to prepare meals. In contrast to the fresh air the Saints had enjoyed on the boat, there was little air circulation in the bus, and the incessant thumping of the tires as they lurched in and out of potholes made rest difficult.

The travel arrangements had included rest stops in members' homes and meetinghouses along the way. But mechanical problems interrupted the schedule with such regularity that the travelers missed most of their connections. Though they were painfully late, the Saints from Manaus were delighted with the refreshments waiting for them that members in Porto Velho had prepared.

Eventually the roads began to improve, as did roadside facilities. The tired travelers arrived in São Paulo at 4:18 A.M. on the seventh day. No doubt they attached some significance to the journey taking them seven days.

For the next four days, these dedicated members worked in the temple. But it was not work in the sense of labor, so ready were they to rejoice in the spirit of the temple and its blessings. They received their own endowments, were sealed as families, and then performed temple work for others. In addition, many received patriarchal blessings that they would use as a personal Liahona for years to come. Their time in the temple concluded with a special session exclusively for the members of the Manaus stake.

On the twelfth day, they got back onto the bus that had brought them. They carried with them the charge of increased fidelity to the gospel of Jesus Christ. They reflected on the many sessions they had attended, the sealings performed, the temple work they had done.

All too soon the world and its challenges intruded. The bus broke down, and they again missed connections. Before crossing an old, fragile bridge, everyone exited the bus to lighten the load. A few sturdy timbers were laid to strengthen the bridge, and the bus crept slowly across.

On Sunday they attended a stake conference in Campo Grande, where those presiding dedicated a portion of the meeting to the courage and determination of the "temple Saints" from Manaus.

When they reached Humaita, they again boarded the boat for the final stage of their journey. The days on the river were uneventful and peaceful. Their journey had taken sixteen days. As President Kimball had prayed, holy angels had guarded them and the spirit of the temple had presided over their souls.

> *I have seen your labor and toil in*
> *journeyings for my name.*
> Doctrine and Covenants 126:2

# WHAT HAVE I COME TO?

"What have I come to?" Kate Marshall wondered as she looked out the train window at the unfamiliar countryside speeding by. The scenes outside were so different from home. Tunnels of snow, drifts in every direction, open, rugged countryside. "What have I come to?" she mused again and again.

This gentle woman had left her home and friends in Worthing, on the south coast of England, to travel with her husband to join their war-bride daughter and young family in Orillia, Ontario, Canada. It was 1948.

Resilient and determined, she quickly became part of the community. If Canada was to be her home, she would make herself comfortable with the people, their traditions, and their way of doing things. That attitude eventually led her to read the Book of Mormon given her by friends two years earlier. When the missionaries knocked on her door, she was ready to be baptized. "I knew the Book of Mormon had to be of God," she testified. "A young boy like Joseph Smith could not have made it up."

Her exuberance for the gospel was not shared by her husband, however. A full eight years passed before he joined the Church.

The Church had little visibility in the community at that time. The few converts met in the members' homes, and Sister Marshall always reveled in "the strong spirit there." By 1957 the Orillia Branch was organized, and for years they rented the hall of an athletic club for their meetings. Sister Marshall went early to empty ashtrays and air out the rooms. In the summer months, she brought fresh flowers from her garden to add some color to the otherwise dim setting.

Sister Marshall was always doing what needed to be done. When the branch held bake sales, her chocolate cake was one of the first to go. At a branch rummage sale, she had to rescue her coat from the hands of an interested buyer.

As a visiting teacher, Sister Marshall was a legend. She walked many miles to the homes of sisters, usually alone. Many times she and others laughed "that only Mormons or the English would be out on a day like this." At age eighty, she climbed ladders to see the renovations in progress at the homes of those she visited. In her nineties, she still did her visiting teaching with precision and a strong sense of purpose. Not until she was ninety-nine and in a wheelchair did she accept the idea that her role as a visiting teacher was now to encourage others and looking forward to their visiting her.

She never lost her love for England nor did she lose touch

with her family and friends who were there. Her brother and his wife joined the Church through her influence. She and her husband were sealed in the London England Temple. Later she attended the Toronto Canada Temple, the temple of her adopted home. For it was in Canada that she found the gospel. "What have I come to?" she often asked, and then she answered herself, "I have come to Zion."

> *Thou hast with unwearyingness declared the word,*
> *which I have given unto thee.*
> Helaman 10:4

# TEN MILES OVER THE WELSH HILLS

On Sunday, 12 September 1993, the Thanet Branch of the Maidstone England Stake met at the Broadstairs Nursing Home to celebrate the eighty-ninth birthday of Agnes Griffiths Giles. A widow for twenty-five years, she had been "a stalwart. Her testimony is unshakable, and she has been an outstanding example of dedication and endurance for nearly a century," said the high priest group leader who led the celebration.

Agnes had learned early in her life to prize the gospel. The members of the Griffiths family were the only Latter-day Saints in Abercarn, Monmouthshire, Wales, so Agnes attended church meetings in her family's small home, which was owned by the city council. Others who were interested in the gospel sometimes attended the meetings. But when the daughter of a prominent member of another church in the village seriously began investigating the LDS Church, persecution was poured out on the family. Articles filled with untruths were published in the newspaper. Rumors were rampant. The council, persuaded that the Mormons were evil, ordered the family to halt church services in their home or be evicted. Though the Griffiths family valued their Sunday worship, they also felt their responsibility to obey, honor, and sustain the law. (See Article of Faith 12.)

The nearest branch was in Varteg, ten miles over the Welsh hills. If they wanted to attend church, they'd have to go there. So, very early the next Sunday, the Griffiths family walked to the top of Llanuack Mountain, down to the Nafodrynys Valley, back up Pontypool Mountain, and finally into Varteg.

To keep up their spirits and their pace, the family sang and recited scriptures. Often it rained, and they arrived at church soaked to the skin. The Saints in Varteg dressed them in dry clothes while theirs were hung up to dry.

For many months the family made their trek to church, much like earlier pioneers who also had to leave their homes to practice their religion. Then one day a letter to the city council arrived from Salt Lake City:

"On my desk is a clipping from the South Wales *Argus* which conveys the information that recently your honorable body took action against one of your fellow townsmen, depriving him of the right to hold religious services in his home. The only reason for such arbitrary action was that 'He is a Mormon.'

". . . But have you gone far enough? Are you now aware of the fact that the gentleman in question is still offering prayers in his home? Have you not been informed by the 'society for the promulgation of slander,' or whatever that certain organization is called that the tenant and his children against whom you are passing a special ordinance are rendering thanks to their God every night and morning?

"Why not complete your work by demanding that such prayers be not offered in a house that belongs to a Christian city council? If you have the right to prevent his singing hymns and of speaking in the presence of his family, and of friends, of the grace and goodness of God, you also have the right to order him to cease his prayers 'because he is a Mormon.' Therefore, he must be deprived of the most cherished of traditional privileges."

Elder David O. McKay, author of the letter, closed with, "To judge either a man or a people so unjustly is unbecoming a body of intelligent men."

The council tabled the letter, but it was published in the local newspaper, and the community responded. A women's club invited Brother Griffiths to speak to their meeting, and his testimony prompted them to support the right of the Griffiths family to hold worship services in their home. The city council rescinded their action, and the Griffiths family began again to hold their meetings at home.

Just as persecution had solidified the testimonies of many early pioneers, the experience of the Griffiths family proved a blessing for them as well. Agnes never questioned her testimony, always sharing with others the truths she had learned so well as a child.

*For where two or three are gathered in my name,*
*there am I in the midst of them.*
Matthew 18:2

# IF I DIE FOR THE RIGHT REASON

Eric Zulu, a soft-spoken, gracious, and patient man was an unlikely candidate for a confrontation. Shortly after joining the Church, he was called as president of the Kwa Mashu Branch in a black township near Durban, Africa. He, like other pioneers before him, faced unrest in his community and threats to his safety.

The unrest that plagued his community edged closer and closer to violence. A leader of a political group involved in the fighting needed a place to hold a rally. Because of his fierce and intimidating presence, he was used to having his requests granted. Quickly. He did not expect a challenge when he approached President Zulu about using the Latter-day Saint chapel.

He also had not expected to find obedience a more powerful

motive than fear. Aware of the policy that Church buildings were not be used for political purposes, President Zulu responded to the request with a firm no. He felt keenly his responsibility to protect the sanctity of the small chapel.

The political leader, used to violence as a means to resolve issues, threatened the young Church leader. "We will destroy your house, burn your car, and then we will kill you."

President Zulu stood firm and levelly replied, "If I am dying for the right reason, it's okay."

Then President Zulu was inspired to open his *Melchizedek Priesthood Handbook* and show the political leader the policy. "If you were in my place, what would you do?" The man looked at the handbook and then at President Zulu. He agreed with the young leader's decision, respected his resolve, and left to organize elsewhere.

> *Be ye stedfast, unmoveable, always abounding*
> *in the work of the Lord.*
> 1 Corinthians 15:58

# CALLED TO BE THE BISHOP

The years after World War II were difficult in Germany. It was 1948, and fourteen-year-old Peter Boehme added to his family's income by carrying suitcases and bags from the railroad station to travelers' homes. Peter and his family had survived the war, though they lived in Dresden, which had been heavily bombed by the Allied Forces.

On this day, he picked up the bags of two men dressed in suits and asked their destination. They explained to Peter that they had traveled from Cottbus to conduct a conference for The Church of Jesus Christ of Latter-day Saints and they had no overnight accommodations arranged. Peter took them home to stay in his family's spare room, and the two men, district president Fritz Lehnig and Otto Sasse, converted the whole family. Peter, his parents, his brother, Lutz, and his two sisters, Ingrid and Helgard, were baptized in a Dresden stream.

Three years later, at age seventeen, Peter fled to West Germany when the tensions between East and West intensified. Wanting to start a new life, he emigrated to Australia and lived for some time in the outback of Queensland before contacting Church members in Brisbane. In 1956 he accepted a call to serve a building mission in that area.

Then he married. He and his wife, Ann, began looking for property where they could build a home. One day, as they headed for the Gold Coast Hinterland, a fierce storm forced them to stop in the town of Beenleigh. Waiting for the weather to clear or at least improve, they decided to look around at property for a home. Peter and Ann put down a deposit to secure a plot they liked. They intended to go home and pray about whether they should purchase the property.

That night Peter dreamed that he was called as bishop of Beenleigh Ward. In the morning he told Ann of his dream. She teased him that it was probably more an aspiration than an inspiration—after all, only three LDS families lived in Beenleigh. They themselves attended the Eight Miles Plains Ward, about a fifteen-minute drive from Beenleigh.

But the next night, Peter had the same dream again. This time, the dream included a congregation of members and a chapel being built in the area of Beenleigh. The third night, he again dreamed of serving as bishop of the Beenleigh Ward. This time the Beenleigh Ward was so large that members were being moved from that ward to form yet another.

Peter and Ann could no longer make light of the dreams. They obeyed the prompting and agreed to purchase the property. When they applied for a loan, they could show only a few dollars in their account, and the bank manager doubted that the loan would go through. Nevertheless, three hours later, they had received a loan. The land was theirs.

A year later, on 18 December 1978, the Church created the

Beenleigh Branch, and Peter Boehme was called to serve as the branch president. There were 29 active members. Five years later, the branch had grown to 245 members, and on 27 November 1983, the Beenleigh Branch was made into a ward. Franz Herman Peter Boehme was called as bishop. The following year, on 14 October 1984, the ward dedicated a newly built chapel.

Church membership in the area continued to grow, and by 1986 the Marsden Ward was formed from the Beenleigh and Eight Mile Plains First and Second Wards. The new ward met in the Beenleigh Chapel until its own chapel was completed in 1988.

The prophetic dreams of Peter Boehme had been fulfilled in only a little more than ten years.

*I did obey the voice of the Spirit.*
1 Nephi 4:18

# DID YOU SAY OUTER MONGOLIA?

The stake president of Dr. C. DuWayne and Alice Cannon Schmidt smiled at the two of them as they walked into his office. "Will you accept a call to serve in Outer Mongolia?" he asked. "Of course," the Schmidts replied, "if the Lord has called us, we will serve. But tell us, where are we really going?" The President's answer was sobering, "You're going to Mongolia."

Members of The Church of Jesus Christ of Latter-day Saints have been called to missions in distant lands since missionary work began in the late 1830s. The pioneers who crossed the plains came from foreign lands to settle a Zion they had never heard of and no one had ever seen. They came with faith, courage, patience, and humility.

To the Schmidts, as to most in the Western world, Mongolia was the last stop before outer darkness. Landlocked between Siberia on the north and China on the south, Mongolia is an enigma. Genghis Khan, rampaging Mongols, and frigid winters on the stark plains were all the Schmidts could picture. They were not alone in their bleak views. For decades, Mongolia has not been involved in international markets or in academia. Cultural treasures have not been exhibited, nor have they fielded strong Olympic teams. In fact, Mongolia had been a vassal state until the collapse of the Soviet empire. Now Mongolians were free to choose, and they were choosing to change.

They needed help. Church officials in Asia approached Mongolian government officials, offering to provide couples whose professional training could be used to redirect the Mongolian higher education system and certain specialty areas, medicine in particular. Mongolia opened its doors to six couples, the first missionaries to Mongolia from The Church of Jesus Christ of Latter-day Saints as far as any records show.

In September 1992 Kenneth H. Beesley and his wife, Donna, received the first call to serve in Mongolia. He was formerly president of LDS Business College in Salt Lake City. Joining the Beesleys were Richard and Anna Harper, Stanley and Marjorie Smith, Royce and Jane Flandro, Gary and Barbara Carlson, and DuWayne and Alice Schmidt. Within six months they were joined by six young elders and then six more.

They learned that Mongolia is a sparsely populated country with about 2.2 million people in an area about the size of Alaska. More than one-fourth of the people live in the city Ulaanbaatar, where the Church service couples were placed. There are only two other cities of any size, Darhan and Erdenet. More than two-thirds of the people move about the countryside, just as their ancestors did, with their camels, sheep, goats, yaks, horses, and cows. In fact, animals outnumber the people twelve to one. Their homes, called yurts, are portable felt tents with a stove in the middle for heating and cooking. Yet government figures report a literacy rate in Mongolia of 90 percent, extremely high for such an otherwise underdeveloped country. Half the people still dress in their native clothing, although many in the city have adopted western styles. Animals of all kinds—elk, cows, pigs, and goats—

roam city streets, and neighborhoods offer a mixture of yurts and the stark concrete apartments built by the Russians.

The experience in Mongolia was pioneering in every way. Brother Schmidt described it like this:

"We arrived in the middle of a Mongolian winter on February 19, 1993, joining three other pioneering couples. Elder Beesley greeted us at the Ulaanbaatar airport and drove us through the snowy city to our adequate, but cool, third-floor apartment. Our flat had a basic kitchen, bathroom, living room, dressing room and two bedrooms, one of which we used as a study and examination room. The furniture was limited to essentials, and the bare, orange painted floors projected a Chinese mood."

The missionary couples were aided in their efforts by Church General Authorities. On 15 April 1993, Elder Neal A. Maxwell of the Quorum of the Twelve Apostles dedicated the country for the preaching of the gospel. He asked the Lord to bless the nation and people of Mongolia that they might be able to maintain their independence and find ways to better their economy.

The missionaries were needed and welcomed. Elder John Carmack of the Area Presidency reported, "It is to the point where the government is asking if there is any way we can send more missionaries." The couples assisted government leaders and educators in the transition from a Russian way of doing things to a western style. They worked in consolidating the university structure, planning curriculum and teaching English.

Dr. Schmidt worked in the medical school. It was not at all like home. "The environment, with the limited and primitive resources of the only medical school in Mongolia, was depressing and challenging. However, we found the faculty anxious to learn and grateful for anything we did for them."

He rewrote the Mongolian text on pulmonary medicine, presented a gift of essential medical textbooks, established ties with the American College of Physicians and other medical associations and such world-health organizations as the Red Cross, and prepared weekly lectures for medical school faculty and students. Sister Cannon taught English.

These missionaries were allowed to talk openly about their religion and hold services. Dr. Schmidt explained how the door was opened for the people of Mongolia to learn of Jesus Christ and his Church:

"When we arrived in Mongolia, Togtohyn Enkhtuvshin, associate professor in the Mongolian National University of Arts, was studying at a university in East Germany. There he met James K. Lyon, Ph.D., who was on sabbatical leave from a university in San Diego. A relationship of trust was established. Enkhtuvshin was taught the gospel and baptized while in Eastern Europe. Upon his return to Ulaanbaatar, Enkhtuvshin assumed he would be the only member of the Church in his country; however, two days after returning to Mongolia, his eyes fixed on two young men who looked like Mormon elders. Enkhtuvshin called out to the elders in German. They responded because Elder Hansen spoke German. At that time none of the elders had learned Mongolian and Elder Hansen was the only missionary who could speak German. They spontaneously felt the joy of finding each other and the brotherhood of the gospel. It is our conviction that the Lord inspired these meetings. Since that time Enkhtuvshin's wife and five children have joined the Church. He is now first counselor in the Ulaanbaatar Branch, and it is growing."

When the Schmidts were released in July 1994, 114 people had joined the Church in Mongolia. Six months later that number had jumped to 240. The Schmidts left their Mongolian service with strong testimonies: "We repeatedly witnessed the hand of the Lord assisting us to reach our righteous objectives. We were often guided in teaching medicine and English and sharing the gospel. Alice and I felt that we accomplished more good for more people in those eighteen months than I probably achieved during my entire thirty-two years of medical practice."

> *Look unto me, and be ye saved, all the ends of the*
> *earth: for I am God, and there is none else.*
> Isaiah 45:22

# GIVE ME TILL MIDNIGHT

For many years George Boyd worked for the LDS Church Building Department in Canada. His service in the London Ontario Stake was "full of spiritual experiences" that he recorded in his journal "because of what I consider the tendency to believe that miracles are a thing of the past."

He would not have described himself as a pioneer, and yet his reliance on the Lord reflected the qualities of humility and obedience that helped the early Saints settle remote areas and build their temples with simple tools. For most, their efforts were quiet contributions; they were faithful and obedient members doing their part.

Meeting with others who also had responsibility for the building of the Church in their communities, Brother Boyd discovered that many of their needs were the same—to be blessed personally and "to control the weather."

Brother Boyd wrote in his journal: "When helping at the Etobikoke Stake Centre in Toronto my family was called to fill a building mission. We received $250 a month living allowance to buy food and clothes etc., so we decided to sell our home. The ward pitched in with their paintbrushes on the exterior of the house during the weekend, and Monday morning early I left for my work in Toronto. Joyce walked over to the local hardware store to buy a 'For Sale' sign to put in the window of the house. On the bridge coming home a neighbor stopped her and said, 'I hear your house is for sale. I'll buy it.' So the sign never got put in the window.

"We went out the next week and bought a used three-bedroom house-trailer and had it towed to our first mission project, a chapel to build in Barrie, Ontario [Canada].

"We had started late in the season so I had some catching up to do. We needed good weather. We had a drought in Ontario that year so we were able to press ahead. We got to the stage where we were readying to pour the floor of the building. As I was in my little shack studying the blueprints the radio was on and they announced that the farmers were going to hold a special prayer service for rain. There I was praying for continued good weather, and the farmers needed rain. I gave it some thought and then prayed, 'If Thou wilt give me till midnight on Monday, then the rain can come.'

"We poured the concrete and machine trowelled it and then everybody went home exhausted. I stayed to hand finish. By midnight it was still not quite finished, and a fine mist started to fall. By one o'clock the rain was full and steady, but the floor was good and the rain was a good curing agent. I was soaked and aching, but happy. I went home, took a hot bath, and went to bed.

"The next day the farmers acknowledged the answer to their prayers, and I acknowledged the answer to mine."

*And the prayers of the faithful shall be heard.*
2 Nephi 26:15

# ANGELS IN THE MURAL

Russia, as a country, has always had a place in the kingdom of God. In June 1843 the Prophet Joseph Smith called Orson Hyde and George J. Adams to serve in Russia. That, he said, would bring about "some of the most important things concerning the advancement and building up of the kingdom of God in the last days, which cannot be explained at this time." (Joseph Smith, *History of The Church of Jesus Christ of Latter-day Saints,* 7 vols. 2d ed. rev., ed. B. H. Roberts [Salt Lake City: The Church of Jesus Christ of Latter-day Saints, 1932–51], 6:41.)

Though Elders Hyde and Adams never served in "the vast empire" of Russia, the Prophet Joseph's intent and the Lord's will was clear. The gospel was to be preached to the Russian people.

Nearly 150 years later a missionary force finally entered that nation. For half of the twentieth century Russia had been closed to the rest of the world. Belief in religion, even the traditional Russian Orthodox Church, was considered subversive by the Communist government. But in 1985 the Russian government began to remove some barriers. Five years later, in July 1990, Dr. Gary Browning, a professor of Russian language and literature at Brigham Young University, and his wife, Joan, were called to direct the Finland Helsinki East Mission, which had responsibility for Russia and several of its neighbors. The Brownings were joined by their three children: Betsy, Katie, and Jon. By this time, several branches were flourishing in Russia, and several hundred Russian citizens had joined the Church.

Missionaries faced obvious obstacles, among them the rich heritage of the Russian Orthodox Church on one hand and seven decades of state-mandated atheism on the other. But the Spirit had prepared people to hear the gospel and the work began in earnest. President Browning came to fully understand the words of Brigham Young, who said, as he surveyed the efforts of the pioneers in the Valley: "We have accomplished more than we expected . . . the blessings of the Lord have been with us." (Thomas Bullock Journal, 8 Oct. 1847, LDS Church Historical Department.)

When he returned to BYU in 1993, Dr. Browning described a singular moment for him, one in which he saw clearly the power of obedience in furthering the work of the Lord. That moment had come in a meeting on 23 February 1991:

"It had been a considerable trek from Moscow member-missionary work by Americans in early 1990 to the arrival of the first six full-time missionaries in October of 1990 to the organization of the first official Russian Moscow branch in March of 1991, to the establishment of fifteen Russian-speaking branches that February. On February 21, 1993, more than five hundred members and friends were seated comfortably in the newspaper-publishing house Izvestia Building in downtown Moscow across the street on one side from the famous statue of Pushkin, Russia's most beloved poet, and on the other from McDonald's, a must-visit cultural mecca for Western tourists.

"The fifteen branches had just been organized and their presidents sustained. Now the ten new branch presidents were bearing brief testimonies. Most of us were enjoying a particularly delectable spiritual feast. When the eighth or ninth president began speaking, I started to review in my mind the main points of my talk, which would conclude the conference.

"I was prepared to speak on the blessings of attending a large established ward of the Church, as I had done as a youngster living in what was for me the comparative metropolis of Pocatello, Idaho. I would recall our full Church program and lovely meetinghouse, like our Pocatello building with that inspiring mural on the wall behind the podium. The mural depicted heroic pioneers crossing the plains, struggling and, on occasion, disheartened but attended always on the journey by unseen angels. Maybe these pioneers could not see the angels, but every week I and others saw them plainly about the pioneers' heads, and I learned well the lesson that a loving Heavenly Father is aware of our burdens and strengthens us just enough to bear them. And I would draw a parallel to the Moscow pioneers crossing to their eagerly anticipated spiritual Zion.

"Then I wanted to emphasize how much I learned and benefitted in other ways from living during my junior and senior high school years in the small northern Idaho town of St. Maries, where our fledgling branch of the Church met in a humble, two-room Grange hall, similar to the facilities of many of the new Moscow branches. As a teenager there, I had the opportunity to serve with Weldon and David Tovey, two other very young men, in the Sunday School presidency and to grow through the warm encouragement of humble, generous Saints who overlooked our inadequacies and loved us for what we were and what they believed we could become.

"As I was mentally reviewing these and other points, suddenly and unexpectedly I received an intimation, as though a sensation filled my consciousness and in an instant encompassed my whole being. I no longer thought about my talk or listened to the speaker.

"I felt a distinct and powerful impression that the spirit of the Prophet Joseph Smith was with us in this historic meeting. I believe for a moment my spirit felt his spirit of youthful buoyancy, joyful enthusiasm, and expansive vision. As I reflected on this feeling, I realized that, in 1993, 150 years had passed from the 1843 appointment of the first missionaries to Russia and that this day of fulfillment must be an occasion for heavenly rejoicing and grateful recognition of the efforts of so many who over fifteen decades made the emergence of the Church out of obscurity a reality in Russia."

> *Teach one another . . . and practise*
> *virtue and holiness before me.*
> Doctrine and Covenants 38:23–24

# ONLY WHEN IT IS CONVENIENT?

Hidemasa Yatabe knew something about making lonely, difficult decisions. The only member in his family, Hidemasa had joined The Church of Jesus Christ of Latter-day Saints while he was a young boy. He was an accomplished gymnast, a member of the elite All-Japan gymnastics team, and had the opportunity to compete in his sport at the highest levels in national and international competitions. Hidemasa had prepared for that opportunity his whole life.

But he had also prepared himself to serve the Lord. He had been blessed with a testimony. He had had the great honor of having Elder Dallin Oaks of the Quorum of the Twelve Apostles visit him in his home. Elder Oaks had blessed Hidemasa that he would serve a mission.

Now, two years later, Hidemasa sat in a stake conference meeting for all the young men of the Tokyo Japan East Stake to hear a special challenge. Hidemasa will never forget that day, 5 February 1989. "Every worthy priesthood bearer should go on a mission," Elder Oaks said firmly. "It is his responsibility."

The words had great significance to Hidemasa. He had heard that challenge given to him personally two years before. But how could he go? To go would be to abandon his future in gymnastics. To serve a mission would mean giving up his place on the gymnastics team. And this wasn't just a local club; this was his country's premier team. He had worked his whole life to have such opportunities.

His thoughts were not only for himself. "The university had only a few gymnasts and our success was based on team members dedicating a great deal of time practicing together. We even ate together. We became as one technically, mentally, and emotionally. The loss of even one member of a team like that disrupts the entire team. So although I always wanted to go on a mission, I wasn't sure how I could leave the team," he reasoned.

But Hidemasa did not reject the apostle's counsel. He simply set it aside for about six months as he became consumed with his studies and his gymnastics. He was focused on earning the chance to attend the All-Japan Gymnastics Championship.

During that time, though he was committed to his sport, Hidemasa was distracted. The words of Elder Oaks rang in his ears.

"As I began to prepare mentally and physically for a future world-class competition, my desire to serve a mission became stronger and stronger. After the student championship, I was interviewed by my bishop and stake president."

In the interview the stake president spoke frankly. "If you plan to go on a mission only when it is convenient for you, perhaps the Lord might bless you only when it is convenient for him."

Hidemasa determined to send in his missionary papers right away.

But how to tell his team? How to explain he had a spiritual witness that was stronger than a perfect 10? Gymnastics, with all its personal effort and performance, is a team sport. He knew they, too, were counting on him. Announcing his decision was one of the most difficult moments of his life. An outcry went up from his teammates. How could he even consider abandoning their efforts at this time? This event would be for his teammates the culmination of their years of effort, too! And he was leaving!

Some teammates accused him of hurting their chances to win; they scorned his decision as selfish and one-sided. "Religion should make people happy," they said, "so why are you making us suffer!"

"I was grateful for the support the team members had given me in my athletic career," Hidemasa said. "I didn't want to disappoint them. Without their help, I would not have achieved what I did. For me to leave for a mission meant that I would destroy all that we had worked together to build. I knew exactly how they felt. It was painful."

But Hidemasa stood firm.

He looked to then-prophet Ezra Taft Benson for guidance, and he found it in a general conference address: "One of the most difficult tests of all is when you have to choose between pleasing God or pleasing someone you love or respect. . . .

"We should give God, the Father of our spirits, an exclusive preeminence in our lives. . . . "

*"The great test of life* is obedience to God." (In Conference Report, Apr. 1988, 4–5.)

Hidemasa knew he was right. He yearned to share his testimony of the gospel and his understanding of serving God first, but his teammates were in no frame of mind to listen.

He returned to the gym for his last day of practice, only to be humiliated by the coach: "This is a training area for athletes and not a place for you. Gather up all your belongings and get out."

As he walked out of the gym that last time he received a special witness from the Lord. He wrote in his journal: "My life as an athlete is finished. I will never again step into the gymnasium as a competitor. At that moment, I realized that everything I had worked toward had ended, and I could not help but cry. Everything, all the gymnastic life that I had worked so hard to build for the past ten years, including the inter-high school championship and the All-Japan championship, had come to an end.

"With that very poignant realization, I glanced back at the gymnasium. I felt that nothing remained for me there but an empty darkness. Suddenly, tears flowed freely as if to cleanse me. They were not tears of sorrow, but rather tears of gratitude. I felt the deepest gratitude for the many people who had supported, helped, and encouraged me for the first ten years. And I was sincerely grateful to Jesus Christ for his unequaled love and mercy. I rejoiced in the opportunity to demonstrate my love for him."

Hidemasa's decision was again ratified by the Lord when he went to the Tokyo Japan Temple to receive his endowments before leaving for the mission field. "As I entered the celestial room, I felt a great spiritual awakening, and I understood the magnitude of the blessings our Father in Heaven has in store for us. I realized that, eternally, serving a mission was the best thing for me—and for my family, and for my former teammates."

> *He doth require that ye should do as he hath*
> *commanded you; for which if ye do, he*
> *doth immediately bless you.*
> Mosiah 2:24

---

# MAY THY HOUSE BRING BLESSINGS

When the Johannesburg South Africa Temple was dedicated on 24 August 1985, President Gordon B. Hinckley prayed, "May the presence of thy house . . . bring blessings." He also committed that the temple would be "a place of holiness, a haven of peace, a sanctuary from the storms of life." (*Church News,* Sept. 1980, 5.) Seven years later those promises were fulfilled for a humble branch president from Zimbabwe.

Late one Wednesday night Reed J. Webster, second counselor in the temple presidency, received a call from President Ben De

Wet, the other counselor, who was just closing up the building. Brother De Wet reported that the police had just called from their office at the train station to ask that someone from the temple come immediately. A Church member from Zimbabwe who had been traveling thirty-six hours by train had just arrived and was seeking assistance in finding the Mormon temple. The police couldn't understand his dialect except for the words, "Johannesburg temple."

Going out at night, especially to the train station, which was in a particularly volatile part of town, was not recommended. But President Webster contacted another temple missionary, a former president of the South Africa Mission, Maurice Bateman, and the two went to the station. Only the night before those same streets had been the setting for angry demonstrations and violence. As the two drove to the station, they saw police officers, dog patrols, and flashing lights everywhere.

President Webster described what happened when they arrived at the station:

"We parked our car at one entrance to the train station, chained up the steering wheel—regular procedure—and wished we could have chained the car itself to the nearby lamp post. After wandering through the huge dismal building, we finally came upon the police station marked by a single light over the doorway down a dimly lit hall. We gave them the name of the person we thought we were to pick up and out stepped a young, stern-faced man in uniform."

President Webster and Brother Bateman explained they had come in response to a call from someone at the police station. The officer's stern face relaxed as he announced that he had made the call. He had been in a quandary what to do. It wasn't safe to let the man leave the station, yet the language barrier made it difficult to help him find a place to stay. They had offered to take him to his destination, but the late hour suggested no one would be there. That's why they made the call to the temple.

Then Sandalamu Milikafu Chisembe entered the room. A small black man about five feet tall, he radiated a calm that was felt by everyone in the room. He had with him a huge suitcase, which Brother Bateman carried to the car.

President Webster stayed behind for a few minutes to talk to the officer and see that all was in order. "The young policeman began asking questions about our temple and said he would like to visit it. The hustle and bustle of the police station was not too conducive to explaining the gospel and the temple. However, I was able to tell him about a book that I would get to him, which, if he read with pure intent, would teach him more about the Church and the function of temples better than I could at the time. We parted with the typical South African handshake, each feeling he had gained a friend."

Like the pioneers who took newly arrived emigrants into their homes after their trek across the plains, President Webster took Brother Chisembe home to his apartment. As they drove he tried to learn about this gentle man. The two temple workers couldn't understand a word of Brother Chisembe's language, but they could feel his spirit.

Arriving home safely, President Webster began to sort through all the papers that Brother Chisembe had brought with him. In a large manila envelope he had documents of baptism, ordinations, and other Church records for himself and for his family, whom he had left in Zimbabwe. In the packet was a letter he had obviously had someone prepare for him in English. It explained that he was the branch president of the Mufakose Branch, Harare, Zimbabwe. It also described his journey to the Johannesburg South Africa Temple.

"I have come to the temple to seek for spiritual power, for preaching, teaching, and doing all the Lord's work. This is the only way I can communicate with you, because I only talk Chew and I can hardly hear English. I know that there's no other place to get spiritual power other than the temple.

"There are seven townships meeting at Mufakose branch for sacrament meeting. Our number of attendance sometimes goes up but sometimes drops. But I am aware of the problem. When missionaries teach the new members. It is our duties to do home teaching.

"We, the branch president, first counselor and all priesthood find it very difficult to go to members who are far away. Our buses are very unreliable. That's why I have come here to seek for solutions to this problem I am facing at this branch.

"I had only a few dollars but through asking from the Heavenly Father I have managed to come here. From here I will go to Malawi and see two brothers and my daughter because I have sent a Book of Mormon. They also want me to explain about the book so that they can join us.

"(Signed) S. M. Chisembe"

President Webster, a native of Utah, was serving his second assignment in the Johannesburg South Africa Temple. He had seen many faithful Saints sacrifice to attend the temple. But President Chisembe brought new meaning to the scripture "seek ye first the kingdom of God." He spent two days in the temple.

When President Chisembe prepared to leave on the bus, he spoke with a young man who understood his language and was able to fill in other pieces of the story. President Webster learned that Brother Chisembe and his family had sold many of their possessions and skimped on food and other essentials to make it possible for him to go to the temple. He hoped someday to bring his wife and family for the sacred sealing ordinance. And then he bore his testimony, which was full of love and appreciation for the Savior. He concluded with this statement: "So many big businessmen around the building where I work, but Heavenly Father chose me."

*For every one that asketh receiveth; and*
*he that seeketh findeth; and to him*
*that knocketh it shall be opened.*
Luke 11:10

# SOURCES

**FAITH AND HOPE**

"Living the Gospel in Mistolar." Based on Elder Ted E. Brewerton, "Mistolar: Spiritual Oasis," *Tambuli*, Sept. 1990, 10–14.

"When I Say Jump." Based on Eric Shumway, *Tongan Saints: Legacy of Faith* [Laie, Hawaii: Institute for Polynesian Studies, 1991], 229–32.

"No Place for a Temple." As told to the author by Peter B. Trebilcock, architect and former bishop of the Preston England Ward.

"Without the Most Simple Tools." Based on the unpublished account "A Conversion Story: Srilaksaana," by Larry R. White, 1993; Joan Porter Ford and LaRene Porter Gaunt, "The Gospel Dawning in Thailand," *Ensign*, Sept. 1995, 48–55; David Mitchell, "The Saints of Thailand," *Tambuli*, May 1993, 41–45.

"A Better Way." Based on Denny Roy, "Kim Ho Jik: Korean Pioneer," *Ensign*, July 1988, 18–23; "Korea, Land of Morning Calm," *Ensign*, Aug. 1975, 44–46.

"Why Would I Need That?" As told to the author by Marek Vasilkov; *Church News*, 12 June 1993, 7.

"Taking the Gospel Home." Based on Marvin K. Gardner, "Horacio Tulio Insignares: Magnifying the Priesthood," *Ensign*, Aug. 1987, 26–29.

"Seven Times the Note Said Yes." Based on unpublished family history of Kiril P. and Nevenka Kiriakov, 4 May 1991.

"Almost Word for Word." Based on unpublished papers by Marilou D. Paderanga, "Unto the Islands of the Sea," 7 Apr. 1982; Ruben M. Lacanienta, "Perspectives on the Manila Temple," Manila Temple Dedication.

"Wonderful! Wonderful!" Based on "Wonderful! Wonderful! Wonderful!" *Tambuli*, Nov. 1991, 32–33.

"A Small Favor." Based on "Getting Started," *New Era*, Oct. 1989, 35–36; Kahlile Mehr, "The Gospel in Hungary," *Ensign*, June 1990, 8–13.

"I Have Only One Wishes." Based on unpublished letters from Mavis Steadman; Sheridan R. Sheffield, "Asia Area Welcome Mat Is Out in Several Countries," *Church News*, 19 June 1993, 3.

## COURAGE AND DILIGENCE

"I'll Take Care of This." Based on interviews by the author with Jeanne Horne, wife of David Horne, and Joseph Horne, David Horne's brother; Mike Cannon, "Church Gains Recognition in Russia," *Church News,* 29 June 1991; "Two Republics in USSR Are Dedicated," *Church News*, 28 Sept. 1991, 3.

"Inside the Front Cover." Based on unpublished account by Christine Evans Koegler, "Recollections of the Past."

"Nine in the Car." Based on unpublished accounts by Walter T. Stewart and John Gaye provided by Kenya Nairobi Mission president Larry K. Brown.

"Speaking Bahasa." As told to the author by Dr. W. Dean Belnap, missionary to Indonesia and founder of Yayasan Liahona.

"Called to Serve." As told to the author by Marcus Martins; interview with Helvécio Martins by Mark Grover, Harold B. Lee Library, Brigham Young University, Provo, Utah.

"Swim for the Boat." Based on "Members on Isolated Isle Must Rely on Selves, Lord," *Church News*, 10 Sept. 1994, 4.

"Then Came the Velvet Revolution." Based on "Fruits of Faithfulness: The Saints in Czechoslovakia," in *Women Steadfast in Christ* [Salt Lake City: Deseret Book, 1992], 134–47; Carri P. Jenkins, "After the Revolution, the Reemergence of Values," *BYU Today*, Mar. 1991, 30–34.

"'When Ye Are Learned.'" Based on Ann Laemmlen Lewis, "I Found the True Priesthood," *Tambuli*, Aug. 1991, 8–11.

"Jailed for Proselyting." Based on R. Douglas Phillips, Greece Athens Mission president, "Trial and Triumph in Thessaloniki," *Latter-day Digest*, 3 July 1994, 31–34; Elder Tyrel Graves, "Trial and Triumph," *Latter-day Digest*, 3 July 1994, 27–28.

"Remembering Hot Dogs and Sauerkraut." Based on A. C. Christensen and Renee Homer, "Two Pieces of Paper Saved Me," *Ensign,* Feb. 1991, 59–60.

"Whatever Is Needed." Based on Russell M. Nelson, "Drama on the European Stage," *Ensign,* Dec. 1991, 10–11.

## Sources

"You Don't Change Your Religion." Based on "Plowing with Hope," *Ensign,* July 1995, 46–47; interview with India Bangalore Mission president Gurcharan Singh Gill conducted by Roger Keller, 27 July 1994.

"Left to Carry On." Based on Alan Marie, "Leon Fargier: His Faith Wouldn't Go Underground," *Ensign,* Sept. 1991, 29–31.

### PATIENCE AND CHARITY

"Nurse This Little Plot." Based on "Leaving Bitterness Behind Brings Fulfillment," *Provo Daily Herald,* 3 Sept. 1995, E-1; "South African Women's Council Elects LDS as Its Vice President," *Church News,* 23 Nov. 1991, 4; Julia Mavimbela, "I Speak from My Heart: The Story of a Black South African Woman," *Women of Wisdom and Knowledge* [Salt Lake City: Deseret Book, 1990], 61–72; "Saints in South Africa," *Ensign,* Sept. 1986, 48.

"With the Lord Nothing Is Impossible." Based on Christopher J. H. Jones, "Hungry for the Gospel," *New Era,* Mar. 1993, 7–9.

"'A Premeditated Apostate.'" As told to the author by Mary Barton Kirk.

"It All Began with Teakwood Chairs." Based on interview by author with Ng Kat Hing and on Kellene Ricks, "Ng Kat Hing: Hong Kong Pioneer," *Ensign,* Aug. 1992, 50–52.

"Something Changed Rosa." Based on unpublished letter from Sister Jana Seiter, Guatemala Ciudad, 12 Mar. 1994.

"Why Not Us?" As told to the author by Naji Al-Jezrawi of West Bloomfield, Michigan.

"Waiting on the Lord." Based on unpublished account by Cyril West as told to Judith Merrell, 31 July 1993.

"'Notice to Japanese Saints.'" Based on Yukiko Konno, "Fujiya Nara, Twice a Pioneer," *Ensign,* Apr. 1993, 31–33.

"A Promise of Temple Blessings." Based on Douglas F. Tobler, "Alone with God," *Ensign,* Apr. 1993, 50–52; Matthew Heiss and Gerry Avant, "Faith, Courage Sustain German Couple," *Church News,* 11 July 1992, 4–5.

"Tender Apples." Based on Shirleen Meek Saunders, "Whang Keun-Ok: Caring for Korea's Children," *Tambuli,* Oct. 1992, 32–41.

"They Broke Down and Cried." Based on unpublished accounts compiled by Dallas Ryhne and Ritchey M. Marbury.

"Come, Listen to a Prophet's Voice." Based on Yves and Kathleen Perrin, "The Lost Island of Saints," *Ensign,* June 1986, 38–40; in Tahiti Area Conference Report, 1–2 Mar. 1976.

"Filling in the Footings." As told to the author by Hanno Luschin, Lancashire, England.

## HUMILITY AND OBEDIENCE

"Three Sacks of Potatoes." Based on Benigno Patoja, "We Are Very Blessed," *Tambuli*, May 1990, 10–14.

"I Sang to Myself." Based on E. Dale LeBaron, "Pioneering in East Africa," *Ensign*, Oct. 1994, 24–25.

"They Had Come So Far." *Church News*, 13 Mar. 1991, 6; Janet Brigham, "The São Paulo Temple: Story of Sacrifice and Learning," *Ensign*, Oct. 1978, 58–60; "Amazon Again: Site of 1,700th Stake," Gerry Avant, *Church News*, 29 Oct. 1988, 3, 8.

"What Have I Come To?" Based on unpublished paper by Mildred Weatherhead, "An Orillia Pioneer."

"Ten Miles over the Welsh Hills." Based on unpublished letter from David A. Boyson, Tanet Branch high priest group leader, Maidstone England Stake; Thomas J. Griffiths, "Persecution, 1924," *Ensign*, Jan. 1975, 13–14.

"If I Die for the Right Reason." Based on "Eric Zulu of Kwa Mashu," *Ensign*, Feb. 1993, 37.

"Called to Be the Bishop." Based on history of Franz Herman Peter Boehme.

"Did You Say Outer Mongolia?" Based on C. DuWayne Schmidt and Alice Cannon Schmidt, "A Mission Call to Outer Mongolia," *Journal of Collegium Aesculapium*, Spring 1995, 36–45; Kenneth H. Beesley, "The LDS Church and Higher Education in Mongolia," unpublished paper.

"Give Me Till Midnight." Based on George Boyd's Journal, unpublished, 3 Aug. 1993, London Ontario [Canada] Stake.

"Angels in the Mural." Based on Gary Browning, "Out of Obscurity: The Emergence of The Church of Jesus Christ of Latter-day Saints in 'That Vast Empire' of Russia," *Brigham Young University Speeches of the Year, 1993–94* [Provo: Brigham Young University, 1995], 27–35.

"Only When It Is Convenient?" Based on Stephen K. Christiansen, "No Price Too High," *Tambuli*, Feb. 1991, 43–45.

"May Thy House Bring Blessings." As told to the author by Reed J. Webster; "Man of Few Words Radiates Serenity," *Church News*, 4 Jan. 1992; Royden G. Derrick, *Temples in the Last Days* [Salt Lake City: Bookcraft, 1987], 159.

# INDEX